Create Web Pages
Using Dreamweaver 4 and Fireworks 4

Busaba Siriamonthep

Create Web Pages Using Dreamweaver 4 and Fireworks 4

Universal Publishers / uPUBLISH.com
USA • 2001

ISBN: 1-58112-680-8

www.upublish.com/books/siriamonthep.htm

Preface

If you wanted to design a home page during the past ten years, you would have had to be a programmer or be familiar with technology and coding. Now, you can design your own Web pages without coding, if you are a computer user and know how to use certain applications in Windows. Many software companies have made Web site applications very user-friendly. If you have some knowledge of HTML coding, it will be a benefit for you to use Dreamweaver, because it is a professional HTML editor. In Dreamweaver, you can choose to create and edit between either a code or a design view of a document. Although you can use Dreamweaver alone to create Web pages, Fireworks is a good complementary program that can help your Web site become state-of-the-art. Some things that you cannot create in Dreamweaver, such as images and animated graphics, can be constructed with Fireworks. You can also insert and import many media objects into Dreamweaver, but this book will concentrate on Dreamweaver and Fireworks.

You will learn how to use the applications menus, tools, and Panels to create Web pages. Macromedia Dreamweaver and Fireworks also each have a tutorial and Guided Tour that will help you learn how to operate them.

But to construct a Web site, you should also know what content you want published on your Web site. The content should be simple, easy to read, easy to understand, and organized. I will provide suggestions for you regarding Web site planning, design, and management.

Chapter 1, referred to as Web Management and System Requirements, includes the introduction and instructions for Web site design and development for Dreamweaver. You will learn how to devise a plan and design, develop, test, and maintain a Web site, which is the life cycle of Web management.

Chapter 2 will cover Dreamweaver Basics. It will guide you through the steps of creating a local site and learning each menu, tool bars, and toolboxes and Panels. When you know your tools, it will be easier to select and use them efficiently. If you cannot remember every menu, tool, or Panel, you should just try to practice with them regularly. If you are pretty familiar with the menus, toolbars, tools box, and Panels, you can simply use Chapter 2 as a reference while working on the Web pages.

Chapter 3 will teach you how to design a page layout. Design Page Layout is an important part of Web site construction, because it allows you to manage images, text, media objects, and design Web pages. It is like a floor plan for your house. You can manage the number of rooms, the purpose of each room, and also what do you want to put into those rooms. You can select tools like Layout (Cells and Tables), Layer, Frames, and Table.

Chapter 4, titled Managing Assets, Text, Images, and Media Objects, will help you to become familiar with managing assets, inserting and formatting text and objects, and using Panels.

Chapter 5, titled Behaviors, will show you ways to help manage your Web pages. For instance, to create a disjointed rollover image, you must use the Swap Image command in the Behaviors Panel. You can set many types of behaviors using the JavaScript command. In this chapter, you will also learn to how to test and publish your Web site and make sure that your pages are compatible with the browsers.

Chapter 6 is about Fireworks Basics. Fireworks is an application that provides flexible and useful tools for creating graphics. This chapter will show you how to open and save in Fireworks and how the menus and submenus work. Feel free to use this chapter as a reference when needed.

Chapter 7, titled Creating Objects Using Tools, will describe many tools, such as drawing tools and transform tools, that you can use to create vector and bitmap objects. You will learn how to operate those tools in this chapter.

Chapter 8 is about managing Text, Button, and Color. Text editor will allow you to adjust text in your design. You can use drawing tools to create buttons. The stroke, fill, and effect can be applied to both the text and buttons. You can use the effect functions to adjust color, brightness, or contrast, such as Hue and Saturation, and more.

Chapter 9, titled Rollover Image with Hotspot and Slice, will cover hotspot and slice, which are very popular for creating rollover images. You will also learn how to create slice for the swap images using frames.

Chapter 10 will show how to create Rollover Buttons and Animation using Fireworks. Rollover buttons are used regularly to make a link in Web pages. This chapter will guide you step by step on how to add animation to your Web site.

Chapter 11, titled Dreamweaver and Fireworks Together, is will show you how to export graphic files from Fireworks and insert them into a Dreamweaver document

The purpose of this book is to guide you through the process of creating Web pages that will work for you. Remember, practice is important for learning applications. You should read, try to practice with the applications, and create your own practice Web pages and graphics. Then, you will be able to see just how fun creating a Web site can be.

If you have any questions on any topics in this book, you can contact me at jamongarj@yahoo.com. I will be happy to answer your questions. I really want you to get the benefit of my experiences and this book.

Acknowledgement

I would like to thank my husband, Ongarj Siriamonthep, who has always supported and encouraged me to write this book. I also would like to thank my family. Dr.Kanchit Malaivongs is my role model and inspired me to write a book. I appreciate my friends at Software Park Thailand and their contributions and suggestions. A warm, thank you for Mr. Jeff Young at Universal Publishers, who gave me the advice and the opportunity to explore my knowledge. Mr.Samuel and Mrs.Leah Lehrfeld gave me the inspiration to work on the Web projects. Another special thanks for Ms.Lori Fredeking and my friends that contributed their time to review my book. This book could not have been completed without Mr.Pairoj Pugsasin, who designed the artwork for the cover page of this book.

About the author

Busaba Siriamonthep has a master's degree in Computer Science from Hofstra University, New York. She began her career as a programmer analyst, but has always been involved with the technology training industry. She taught Introduction to Computer, Programming, and System Design at Assumption University in Thailand for over nine years, where she was also a systems consultant for many organizations in Thailand. She was a technology transfer officer for Software Park Thailand, to provide support training for the software industry in Thailand.

TABLE OF CONTENTS

CHAPTER 1
INTRODUCTION

A Web site is like a house, a piece of property, or a company that you must plan to setup, otherwise it can be a mess. Before building or buying a house, you would need to know the specifications, such as how many rooms and where to put the bedrooms, kitchen, dining room, leisure room, bathroom, etc. It is the same for a Web site, too. The structure of a Web site must be planned. The link of each page is like a door to each room and stairs to other rooms in a house. The first page is like the reception area. It should be interesting, easy, simple, and guide them to other areas in your site. The structure of the Web pages should be the similar, but you can design each a little differently. Each page should contain information that relates to images and contents. For example, the stove, refrigerator, oven, plates, and glasses should be in the kitchen. The leisure room should have a sofa, a television and a home theater. The decoration will depend on each designer.

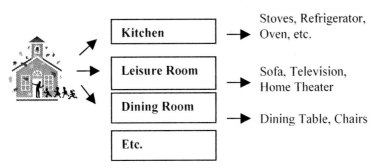

WEB DESIGN AND DEVELOPMENT

The structure of a Web site should match your goals and the purpose of the Web site. You should start with the following questions: why, how, who, what, and when.

Why?
- Why do you want to have a Web site?

This question should be asked first in order to clarify the reason you want to have a Web site, such as for e-business, advertising, information, brand awareness, or education. Then, you can start to plan the structure of your Web site.

How?
- How do you want the Web pages to look?
- How many pages will it be?
- How can you reach target customers or audiences?

You can start to think about design Web pages from this point.

Who?
- Who will be the target customers or audiences?
- Who will be the host server?

This will help you to clarify a plan for your Web site and determine who will visit your Web site, such as teachers, professionals, students, etc. You can then provide more details to the host server, who will provide some means for your Web site to reach out to the world.

What?
- What do people want to know and see on your Web site?

You should also ask yourself this question as if you were a person who will see this Web site.

When
- When do you want to start and publish your Web site?

This will allow you to manage your goals and finish them on time.

Web Management

The purpose of Web site, such as for e-commerce, marketing, services, information, or education, must be determined while planning the Web site.

The life cycle of Web Management is divided into 5 phases.
1. Planning
2. Design
3. Development
4. Implementation and testing
5. Maintenance

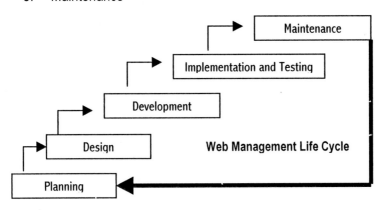

1. Planning Phase

Planning is the first step. This phase will determine the theme of the Web site. The other phases will be smooth, if the planning is done well.

- **Create Structure:** If a Web site isn't well planned, you may have to come back and start it all over again. This can waste your time and cost more money. The better way is to create a good structure of your Web site in the beginning. When you plan for a house, you must survey from many locations. You must have the specifications, such as three bedrooms, two bathrooms, one dining room, one leisure room, two floors, a basement, and placement for a gas heater, and the direction that you want the house to face. Constructing a Web site is very similar, you must determine the pros and cons of other Web sites, how many pages (rooms) you will need, the site plan, security for your site, how can people will access your site, and other considerations, before you begin the design phase. You can improve your work by viewing other examples. For example, if you want to create Web pages about renting a car, you should visit the Web sites of Avis, National, Budget, and other rental agencies to search for information and determine the structures of their Web sites. You should observe the differences and similarities of their sites. Is it easy to find the information you want? Does it take a long time to fill out any forms? The structure is very important. You can redesign and change many things in your pages, but the structure should not be change after you develop the Web site. If the structure does change, it will mean that you will have to go back to the starting point again.

- **Gathering data:** When you know your structure, you can then gather the information, document, graphics, and data needed.

- **Find a host and post your link:** Plan for a host of your site and submit your site to every search engine, if you can. A free host, like Geocities, is just fine for small and personal pages, but they are very slow. A paid host will always be faster than a free host.

- **Navigation**: Navigation is very important. If the visitor has to learn how to navigate your site, it is not a good sign. Navigation should be straightforward and simple, such as an arrow sign, return, next page, etc.

- **Draw Flow diagram:** The diagram should be easy to follow and united, even if you have complicated links in your pages. In the event that you are part of team building the site, all can communicate with the same structure.

Sample Diagram

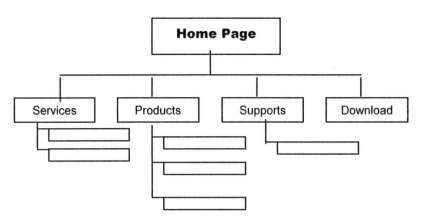

Web sites of many well-known companies have similar structure; they may different in details, industry and designs. Their formats are easy to understand. The suggested Web sites are www.ibm.com, www.bn.com, www.macromedia.com, www.microsoft.com. They group and arrange things in order that customers can find them from menu header.

Example:

To create Web site about foods and recipes, the designer has to plan and create structure of Web site. The recipe of foods will be given out for free. There is a future plan to add the good Thai restaurant in USA and Thailand later on. People can share their homemade recipe within the Web site too. The goal is to share the knowledge on food, beverage, recipes, and herbs for people who love to cook. If some people want to share their recipes, they are invited. They can write e-mail and give information that they want to post on the Web site. The structure of a site must be planned such as how many are Web pages, what will be the content of main page, links, and some plans will be done in the future.

Plan and structure

- To create the home page can be the first thing in a plan and the Web site will be named "Taste of Food"
- The homepage will consist of
  1. Foods
     1.1 Thai food, Chinese Food, Japanese Food, Korean Food, others
        1.1.1 Sub pages will show the list of Appetizers, Main Dishes, Deserts, and Juices
           1.1.1.1 Selected food with the recipe
  2. Herbs
     2.1 List of Herbs
        2.1.1 Selected Herb with detail
  3. Letter from friends
  4. Comment and contact us
  5. Recipe from friends
  6. Advise from chef
  7. Authentic Thai Restaurant (Future Plan)
     7.1 Thailand
        7.1.1 List of Thai Restaurant in Bangkok
     7.2 USA
        7.2.1 State
           7.2.1.1 City
              7.2.1.1 List of Thai restaurants and directions.
- Web pages must be easy and fast to access
- Set Theme of the site like to do it for fun and free, so the host server should be a free host. There are many host servers that provide free spaces for sub domain such as hypermart (http://www.hypermart.net), and freemerchant (http://www.freemerchant.com). However, people can register and pay for their own domain name annually.

Structure Diagram

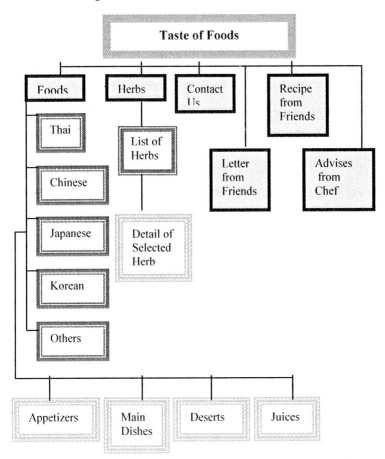

Exercise:

Worldwide Training Company is multi-million dollars company. They train management courses, information technology courses, financial courses and they also have a consultant in each of those field. They want to have their own Web page in order to draw more customers and also announce new courses and activities of the company, what do they need. If you are assigned to do this job, what do you plan for them and please write flow diagram to show your plan. (You can use this exercise to create images, animated images, and Web pages in chapter 2 thru chapter 11.)

2. Design Phase

Designing the site is the second phase. You should organize your data, information, and documents. You should have a flow diagram and expand the diagram in more detail for each page. You should start using Dreamweaver as a tool for the sample pages. You should prepare the images, color of theme, text, and media objects. You should also enjoy your work and view your design as if you are a Web surfer. Do you like what you see? You should solicit comments from your friends or your team. You should also have a comment or a feedback page for people who visit your site. This will allow them to share their ideas with you. The content should also be interesting and up-to-date.

The layout tables and cells in Dreamweaver will help you to organize your page and rearrange cells. You can add more tables and cells (More details in Chapter 3) in that page.

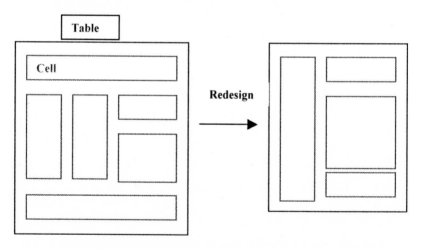

Text, images, buttons and media objects can be inserted into each cell and it will be easy to rearrange.

Note: You can get more design ideas from the Web site. (http://Webdevelopment.developersnetwork.com)

When you have determined your design and layout, you can then create and gather the assets, such as images, text, or media (Flash, Shockwave, Sound, and more). They should be collected in the same group and in the site (More details in Chapter 2). The assets will be available to reuse again and again in that site.

Example:

The structure of "Taste of Foods" is planned. Contents and some graphics are prepared. The sample pages with simple link are created. Graphics that are created using Fireworks will be presented later when development phase is started.

Site name   Main menu

Main menu has many options for visitors to choose. For example if user clicks foods from menu, it will link to the next page that show many kind of foods (Thai, Chinese, Japanese, Korean, and others.) The other menu will be created link as a plan above.

3. Development Phase

Development is the third phase and you must have tools ready to use at this time. However, the tools will only be as efficient as your talent. Most technical people, for example, a programmer, will approach things logically and systematically. Their Web site might be constructed well from a technological aspect, but look ugly. People who surf Web sites want to get information, but also want see a beautiful view. In this phase, you should familiarize yourself with the tools so that your Web site will be visually appealing. You will become familiar with them in Chapters 2 and 3.

4. Implementation and testing

This phase can do parallel with the development phase because you must test them with browsers like Internet explore and Netscape Communicator. You may find errors or incompatible while you develop and you can correct them at that time. If you wait until finish the development, it will be a lot of work because some functions in Dreamweaver may not run well with a browser. We will discuss about items that should be aware of them in chapter 2. When you are ready, you can publish your site.

5. Maintenance

You should establish a maintenance period to ensure quality such as once every four weeks, respond to user feedback, and update the site's information. This will draw more attention from the Web surfers.

System Requirements

The following hardware and software is required to run Dreamweaver

- Netscape Navigator or Internet Explorer version 4.0 or later version.
- An Intel Pentium processor or equivalent, 166 MHz or faster, running Windows 95, Windows 98, Windows 2000, Windows ME, or Windows NT (with Server Pack 3)
- 32 MB of Random Access Memory (RAM) plus 110 MB of available disk space
- A 256-color monitor capable of 800 x 600 pixel resolution
- A CD-ROM Drive

About Macromedia Dreamweaver

Macromedia Dreamweaver is an HTML editor that makes things easy for the user. Before we get started in Chapter 2, you should know about the resources that can help you learn the program after you have the basic knowledge from this book. Macromedia Dreamweaver provides a guided tour, a tutorial, Dreamweaver lessons, and help. You can find these resources from the Help Menu at any time. You can also obtain the Dreamweaver User Guide (printed book) from their Web site at the support center. You can also visit the Macromedia Web site to find the third party like WebSphere from IBM that you can use their tools with Macromedia Dreamweaver and Fireworks, subscribe to the Edge Newsletter, be a member, join the forum, and more.

CHAPTER 2
DREAMWEAVER BASICS
Site Planning and Design

After you install Macromedia Dreamweaver 4 on your computer, you should create a folder (directory) and subfolders (subdirectories) of your site. When you create folder, it will identify itself as a site folder. Your subfolders will group all related data, documents, graphics, and media objects, such as the subfolder, "Images," and store all images that will be used with this Web site and other media in the "Medias" folder. They will be considered as the assets of this site. They should be in one location for one site. If you have two sites, you should create folders for each site separately. You should have a plan with you now. Why? Because when you want to move them to the server site to show the world, you can FTP the main folder that contains all the HTML files, images, and media objects at once. At this point, you should have the images stored in the subfolder, "Images." If you don't organize it, you will have to go back and forth in order to find graphics, designs, and development at the same time. This can be very time-consuming.

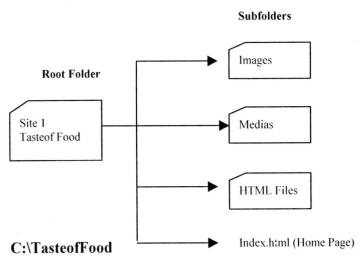

Subfolders

Images

Root Folder

Site 1
Tasteof Food

Medias

HTML Files

C:\TasteofFood

Index.html (Home Page)

Subfolders

Root Folder

Images

Site 2
WWTraining

Other medias

HTML Files
•
•

C:\WWTraining

Index.html
(Home Page)

Example:

(Using "Taste of Foods " project for the practice)

To Create Site Folder for "Taste of Foods"

- Double-click My Computer Icon on desktop.
- My computer dialog box appears.
- Double-click C: Drive.

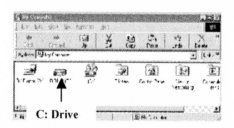

C: Drive

- Choose File > New >Folder.
- Type "TasteofFoods" for new folder.
- This will be a local site for "Taste of Foods".

TasteofFoods

To Create subfolder

- Double-click TasteofFoods Folder.
- The Folder is opened.
- Choose File > New > Folder.
- Type "Images" to name this subfolder.

HtmlFile   Images

- Copy images to put in "Images" folder in order to use for this site.
- Choose File > New >folder.
- Type "HtmlFile" to name subfolder (This folder will be the same level as "Images" folder).

Note: The "index.html" document (Home Page) should be saved in the site folder (TasteofFoods). Other documents should be saved in the "HtmlFile" folder. People can organize and manage the local site differently.

"Templates" folder can be created, if designer want to create many templates for reuse in this local site.

The diagram in window explorer will show folder and subfolder on the left side. If "TasteofFoods" folder is selected, the right side will show all files and subfolders that belong to "TasteofFoods" folder.

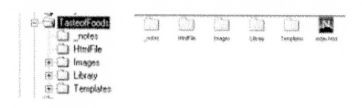

Start Dreamweaver

- Click **Start** menu from the taskbar.
- Move highlight (Blue) to the **Programs** and Click one time at that position to remark them and the right arrow show submenu.
- Move mouse to **Macromedia Dreamweaver 4** and the right arrow show submenu.
- Click to select **Dreamweaver 4**.
- Program Dreamweaver will be launched.

Menu Programs   Menu Macromedia
                       Dreamweaver

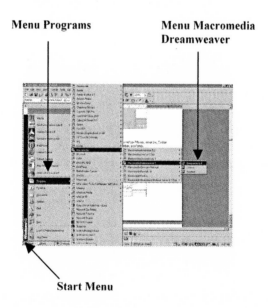

Start Menu

Title bar, Menus bar, Toolbars, Working area, Toolbox, and Panels appear on screen when program is opened.

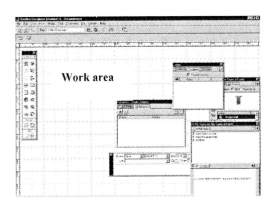

Work area

Title bar

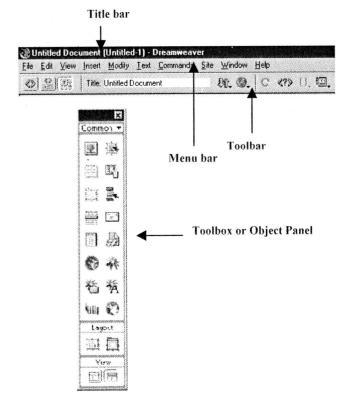

Menu bar

Toolbar

Toolbox or Object Panel

Panels (HTML Styles, CSS, Behavior) →

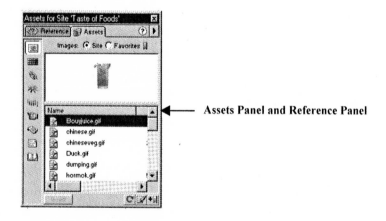

Assets Panel and Reference Panel

Properties Panel
↓

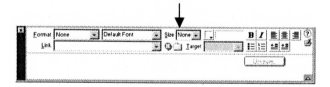

To Set Up a New Site

First of all, the new site in Dreamweaver should be created.
- From Menu bar, choose **Site > New Site.**

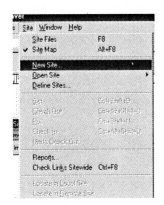

- The Site Definition Dialog box appears.
- Selects the Local site (C: Drive) because all assets and pages are organized in the local site before transfer to the server one time after Web pages are finished.
- Give Name to the Site Name (It should related to the name of the home page).
- Click the yellow folder on the right of Local Root Folder to select the site folder that is already created.
- If the URL is set for being used after completed Web site, you can type it in but we will not go to detail at this point (you can leave it blank for now).
- Keep the check mark on Enable Cache option because the Assets Panel only works if a cache is created.
- Click **OK**.

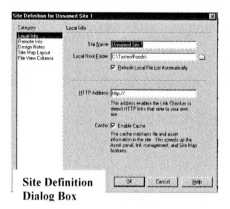

Site Definition
Dialog Box

- The site files window opens; images files in the folder are shown. The home page is created in chapter 3 that will be given the name "index.html".

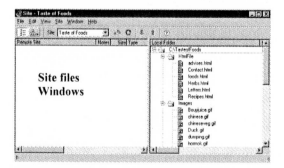

Site files
Windows

- On the right side will show all subfolders and files in site folder.
- To open files from site, double-click a selected file name.

For example: double-click file "index.html", it will open the home page as shown (next page).

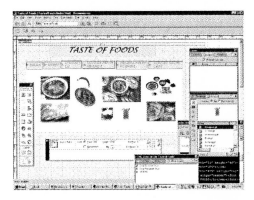

When the homepage (main page) is created, the name "index.html" should be given for system to remember as a first page in a site.

You must define site in order to see the site map.

- Click file name (index.html) in Site Dialog box.
- The Define site Dialog box appears.
- Select site (the blue highlight).
- Click edit button.
- The Site Definition dialog box for selected site appears.
- Select Site Map Layout from Category (with blue highlight).
- Click Yellow folder on the right side of Home Page field to find the index.html and return to this page again.
- Click **OK**.
- The define site dialog box will appear again.
- Click **Done**.

From the toolbar on the Site Dialog box, you will find a Site Map that you can choose to see only a map or a map with files. If you select the map with files, you will see a map diagram on the left side and a list of files on the right.

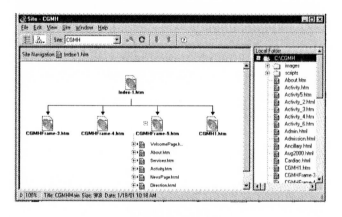

Note: Map is a helpful tool that will show the link diagram of pages in a site.

Menu bar, Toolbar, Tools box, and Panels are guided in this chapter that you can be familiar with the environment of Dreamweaver before starting to build Web pages.

Learn about Menu Bar

Menu consist of the following:

- File
- Edit
- View
- Insert
- Modify
- Text
- Command
- Site
- Window
- Help

File Menu

New means to create the new document, and the short cut key can be used by pressing **Ctrl** and **N** key on keyboard at the same time.
- Choose File > New.

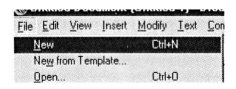

- The untitled Document with blank working area will be open.

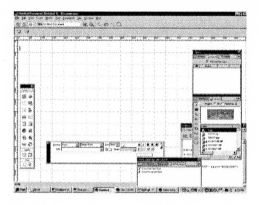

New from Template means to open a new document and using the existing template. Templates have a common structure and appearance. They are useful when all of the pages in a site share certain characteristics such as color, layout and font style.

Note: Creating a template selects **New** document and selects **Save as Template** from menu File.

- Choose File > New from Template.

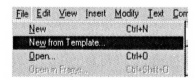

- The Select Template Dialog box will appear.
- Select template (if any) from the existing template. It will open the template file that can be reused.

Note: If template is never be created, the **no templates** will appear in a templates field.

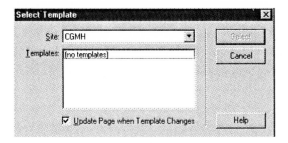

Open means to open the exiting document that is already created, and the short cut key is to press **Ctrl** and **O** key on keyboard at the same time.

- Choose File > Open

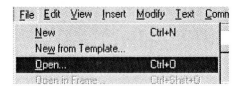

- The open dialog box appears.
- Selects a document to open.

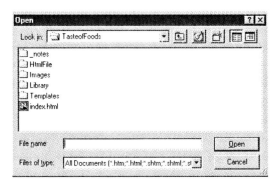

Note: Many documents can be open in different windows and the selected window is the active document that can be worked on it.

Close means to close the open file, the short cut key is to press **Ctrl** and **W** key on keyboard at the same time.

- Choose File > Close

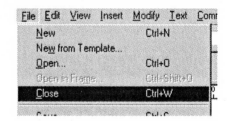

- If document is modified, the dialog box will show and ask to save change or not. To choose yes is to save change. To choose no is to keep the original. To choose cancel is to return to a document again.

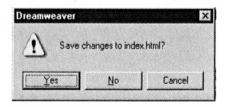

Save, Save As, Save as Template

If it is a new document, to choose **save** or **save as** means to save as. It will show the save as dialog box to give a name for that document.

- Choose File > Save or Save As.

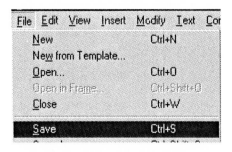

- The save as dialog box will appear.
- Type a name in the file name field and the document will be assigned "htm" extension.

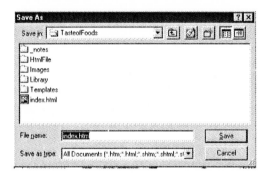

If document is already be saved and give the name, save means to save over the same document even it has been modified and save as means to save as a new document, then a new file name must be assigned.

Save As Template means to save a new document as a template for reuse.

- Choose File > Save as Template.
- The Save As Template dialog box will appear.
- Type a new name of the template in the Save As field.
- Click Save to accept your template name.

Preview in Browser means to check Web pages with the available browsers in a computer. You can check any time while designing and building Web pages. You can press **F12** key on your keyboard and it will run your page on the default browser. You can add more browser by choose Edit Browser List (You can select more browsers that you install in your computer).

- Choose File > Preview in Browser.
- Move highlight to the right and click > IEXPLORE.

To edit browser list

- Choose File > Preview in Browser.
- Move highlight to the right and click > Edit Browser List...

- The preference dialog box will appear and "preview in browser" in Category list will be highlight.
- Click Add (+).

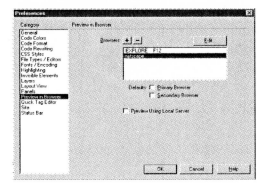

- Add Browser Dialog Box will appear. You have to give the name such as "Netscape".

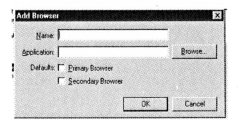

- Click **Browse** to find the application such as "Netscape.exe".

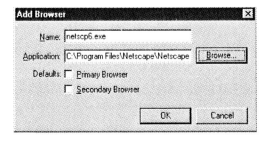

- Click **OK** and the Netscape will be add to list

- Click **OK** to accept the list.
- The Netscape will be in the preview in browser list.

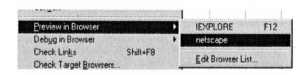

Edit Menu

The edit menu will be used with the working area of a document and consist of the following:

- **Undo**: to undo the last step.
- **Redo**: to redo the last step.
- **Cut**: to cut cell from one location.
- **Copy**: to copy cell from one location.
- **Paste**: to paste cell to another location.

Note: Cut and copy will be used with the paste. If you cut or copy one time, you can paste them many times as you prefer before you assign a new edit command such as cut (another selection).

- **Clear**: to delete the selected content, or cells.
- **Select All**: to select everything in that page.
- **Select Parent Tag**: to select HTML tag.
- **Select Child**: to select sub of HTML tag.
- **Find and Replace**...: to find a text or tag and replace with new text or tag from current document or entire site.
- **Preferences**: to edit the default preferences.
- **Keyboard Shortcuts**: to create your own shortcut keys.

Note: Most applications that run on window have similar edit menu. You can apply how to use them from one to another.

View Menu

You can select view of your choice. If you are familiar with the HTML source code, you can select **Code** view. You can use **Design** view to display a visual representation of your document.

You can split the Document window so that it displays both the Code view and the Design view (**Code and Design**).

While you are working on the document, you can **switch views** any time by pressing **Ctrl** and **Tab** keys on keyboard at the same time.

HTML files has two main sections. They are the **head section** and the **body section**. The body section is the main part of the document, the visible part containing text and images and so on. The head section is invisible, except for the document title, which appears in window title bars in browsers and in Dreamweaver. You should give a title to every page you create.

36

Table View will be discuss with the Toolbox later in this chapter.

If **rulers** and **grid** are selected to show, it will be easy to organize and arrange layout cell and table.

Rulers and Grid

Toolbar

The toolbar contains buttons that will let you toggle between the different views of your document quickly: Code, Design, and both Code and Design view. The toolbar also contains some common commands related to your view selection and your document's status. The Options Menu items (the button located on the right) will change depending on the view you select.

- To view or hide the toolbars, choose View > Toolbar.

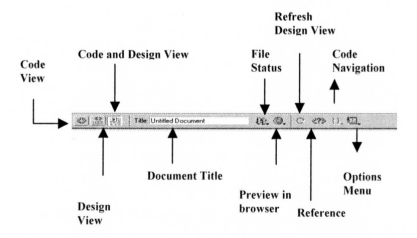

- You can switch between 3 views (Code, Design, or Code and Design view) by click one of the 3 the buttons on the left side of toolbar. If you want to display Code view, you have to click Code View button. If you want to display Design View, You select the Design View button. If you want to display both view, you have to select Code and Design View button.
- When you select view, the option View on Top becomes available in the View menu. Use this option to specify which view appears at the top of your Document window.

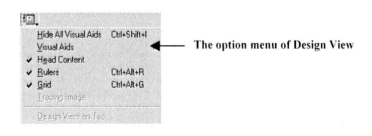

The option menu of Design View

Unhide All Visual Aids will show on the bottom right corner of the screen

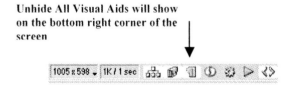

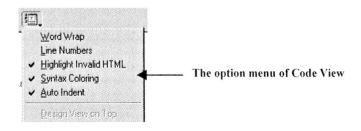

The option menu of Code View

- You can give a title to a new document by typing in the Title field. If the document already has a title, it will appear in this title field.
- You can display the File Status pop-up menu by click the File Status Menu button.
- You can preview or debug your document in a browser by click the Preview/Debug in Browser button and choose one of the browsers listed in the pop-up menu.

- To refresh your Design view, click the Refresh Design View button.
- To access the Reference Panel, click the Reference button. The Reference Panel contains reference information on HTML, CSS, and JavaScript code. (Source is from the Macromedia Dreamweaver help.)
- You can navigate through your code by click the Code Navigation button.

Insert Menu

You can add many objects into your document, such as images, interactive images (Fireworks, rollover, buttons), media (Flash, Shockwave, and so on), tables, layers, frames, e-mail link, forms, date tabular data, and more.

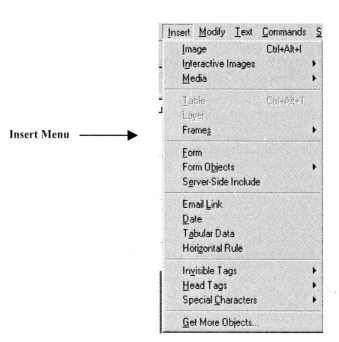

Insert Menu ————————▶

Image

- To add image, choose Insert > Image.

- The Select Image Source dialog box appears.

- You can select image by click the file name from list and click select button to accept your choice.

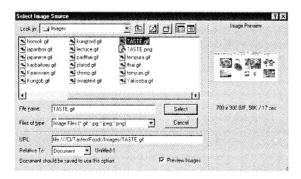

40

- Image will be pasted on the open document.

Interactive Images

- Choose Insert > Interactive Images

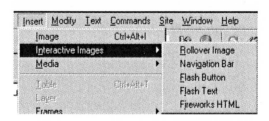

- The pop-up menu will appear, you can select from list.

* Rollover Image
- Choose Insert > Interactive Images > Rollover Image
- The Insert Rollover Image dialog box appears, you can type a new name of image in the Image Name field.
- Browse to find the original image and rollover image

Note: You must prepare images for the rollover before using them.

Original Image
(Sample)

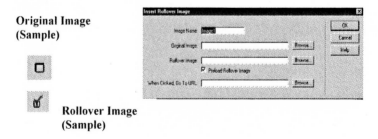

Rollover Image
(Sample)

* Navigation Bar

A navigation bar consists of a set of images whose display will change based on the actions of a user. Navigation bars often provide an easy way to move between pages and files on a site.

A navigation bar element has four states:

Up state will use the image to show while user doesn't move mouse pass the image yet.

Over state means that user move mouse over up image and the image changes to let user know they can interact with it.

Down state show the image after the element has been clicked. If navigation bar still show, it should present that user already selected that navigation before.

Over While Down state should be used to let user know that this navigation bar couldn't be clicked again.

You don't have to include navigation bar images for all four of these states, you can use two states: Up and Down states. You can create a navigation bar, copy it to other pages in your site, use it with frames, and edit the page behaviors to show different states as pages are accessed.

- Choose Insert > Interactive Images > Navigation Bar.
- Type Name in the Element Name field.
- Click Browse to insert the Up Image and Over Image (Down Image and Over while down are the option).

Note: Images should be related together.

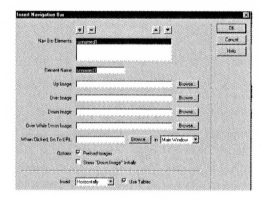

For example:

 Circle light red button will represent up state.

 Circle dark red button will represent over state.

Once you create navigation bar for a document, you can add or remove images by using the modify navigation bar. This will be discussed in the modify menu

* Flash Button

You can insert a flash button that is already included with Dreamweaver or you can get more styles from the Macromedia Web site.

- Choose Insert > Interactive Images > Flash Button.
- The Insert Flash Button dialog box appears.
- You can select from style list and click **OK** or you can click "Get More Style" button to find more style from the Internet.

43

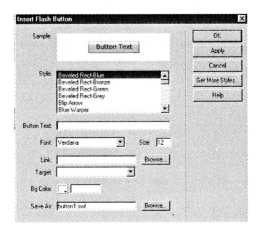

- **Flash Text**

You can create and insert a Flash movie that contains just text. This allows you to create a small, vector-graphic movie with the designer fonts and the text of your choice.

- Choose Insert > Interactive Images > Flash Text.
- Select Font from list, Size, Color for normal and rollover position (they should be different color for example dark blue for normal and light blue for rollover).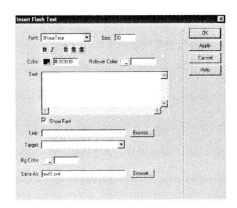
- Type Text in the text field.
- You can browse to link with other page.
- Click **OK** to return to a document.

* Fireworks HTML

- Choose Insert > Interactive Images > Fireworks HTML
- The Insert Fireworks HTML dialog box will appear.
- Browse the html file that create from fireworks
- Click **OK**

Media

You can insert many media objects (Flash, Shockwave, Generator, Applet, Plugin, and ActiveX).

Frame

You can organize Web page by using frames to divide it into multiple HTML pages. For example the top left for logo and top right for company name and address. The left frame below will stand for all menus that will link to other pages. These 3 frames will not be changed (static) when you select from menu (Welcome, About Us, Services, Visitor Guide, Admission, Our Activities, News, Our location, Contact us, and Home) but the right frame (blue) will be changed (dynamic) as your selection.

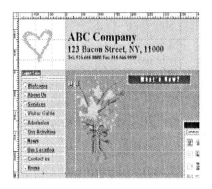 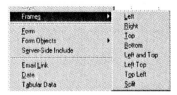

Form and Form Object

You can create and insert a form or a form object, such as a text field, a button, or a check box, to get information from visitors.

- Choose Insert > Form Object > Insert object that you want, one at a time.

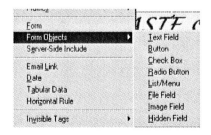

Email Link

You can create email link for visitor to send email to you.

- Choose Insert > Email Link.
- The Insert Email Link dialog box appears.
- Type **Contact us** into a text field.
- Type email address that you want them mail to you into email field.
- Click **OK**.

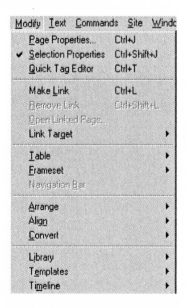

Note: Other menus do not show here, you can find them from Dreamweaver help menu.

Modify Menu

The Modify Menu consists of Page Properties, Selection Properties, Quick Tag Editor, and so on. You can change the set up of many properties and objects at any time here while you are working with document.

- Choose <u>M</u>odify > <u>P</u>age Properties
- The page properties dialog box will appear.
- You can change title in title field, change background color, text color, specify link color and so on.
- Click **OK** after finish modification.

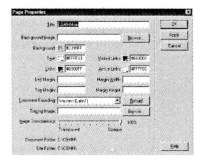

You can modify the library and template for a current page or entire site. Timeline can be used for creating the animation, such as moving an image from left to right.

- Choose <u>M</u>odify > Ti<u>m</u>eline > Add Object to Timeline.
- The Timelines dialog box appears.
- Select image in a layer and drag to time line.
- Preview in Browser to check the animation.

Note: The suggestion is to create animation from fireworks or Flash that will be efficiency and you can insert them to documents, the animation will be flexible and look better.

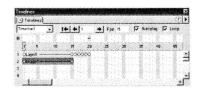

Text Menu

You can set text by using Text menu or properties Panel (will discuss later in this chapter). Text menu consists of the following:

- Indent
- Outdent
- Paragraph format
- Align: Left, Center, Right
- List
- Font: Font Type such as Arial, Lucida Sans, etc.
- Style: Bold, Italic, Underline, etc
- HTML Style: add new style by user
- CSS Style: add new style by user
- Size: number of size such as 2,3,4
- Size Change: increase or decrease size
- Color: Color palette
- Check Spelling

Command Menu

The command menu consists of many functions that can be applied to documents. For example **"Add/Remove Netscape Resize Fix"** should be add to each document for fixing the resize when you use the Netscape browser.

- Choose Commands > Add/Remove Netscape Resize Fix...

49

- The Add/Remove Netscape Resize Fix dialog box appears.
- Click Add (If you want to remove, you can repeat the same step again the Add button will be changed to be Remove button instead).

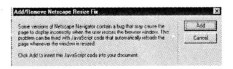

Site Menu

The Site Menu consists of Site Files, Site Map, New Site, Open Site, Define Sites, and so on. This menu will help you to manage the site. We already talked about them in the beginning of this chapter, but we will continue to discuss them later in Chapter 5 for transferring (FTP) your site to the server.

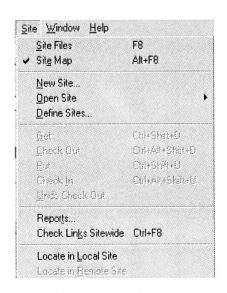

Windows Menu

The Window menu consists of useful Panels, such as Assets, Behaviors, Code Inspectors, and so on. The check mark in the front of the Panel list means that it is open.

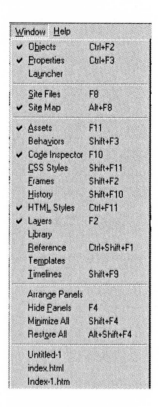

- Choose Window > Assets (Panel in a list).

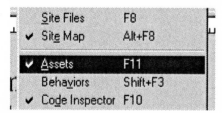

- The Assets Panel appears on the top of working area.
- If you want to open other Panels, you can repeat those steps.

Assets Panel ⟶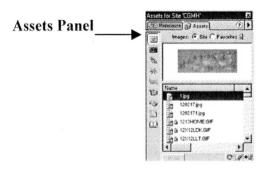

Note: Other Panels will be discussed in Panel Section (Chapter 2).

Help Menu

The Help Menu is useful for user. You can find references at any time, such as Dreamweaver Help, Guided Tour, and Lessons. They are provided with the Macromedia Dreamweaver application. Others, such as the Dreamweaver Support Center, will link you to the Macromedia Dreamweaver Web site.

Tools box

The Tools Box contains buttons for creating and inserting objects, such as tables, layers, and images. There are seven categories for you to choose from: Characters, Common, Forms, Frames, Head, Invisibles, and Special. You can select them from the Insert Menu too. The Object Panel has a Standard and Layout View. If the Layout view is selected, you can use the Layout Cell and the Layout Table button, but the Table and Layer button cannot be used at this stage. If the Standard View button is selected, the Layout Cell and Layout Table button cannot be used.

To show or hide the Tools box, choose Window > Objects.

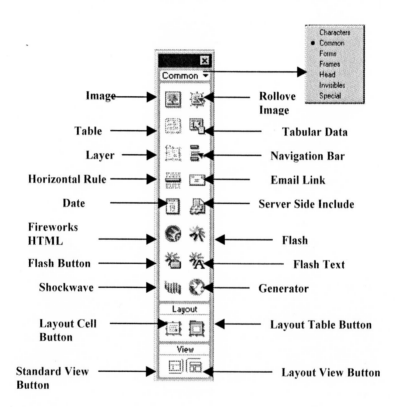

Assets Panel

- To open Assets Panel, choose Window > Assets.

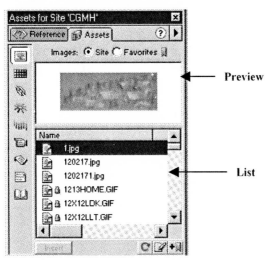

The Assets Panel shows that these media objects are available for documents in your local site. The lists on the left side of the Assets Panel are media objects that are available to be used, such as images, colors, URLs, Flash, Shockwaves, movies, scripts, and templates. For example, if you click on the image button on the left side of Assets Panel, images in this local site will appear. You can drag and drop images from the Assets Panel to your current document. The preview will show a selected image file. You can reuse images with documents in this local site.

History Panel, Layer Panel, Frame Panel

- To open History Panel, choose Window > History.
- To open Layers Panel, choose Window > Layers.
- To open Frames Panel, choose Window > Frames.

The History Panel will show you all the steps that you can perform in an active document. The Layer Panel will show all the layers you have active in the document. If you create frames, it will be shown in the Frames Panel.

Behaviors Panel

- To open Behaviors Panel, choose Window > Behaviors.

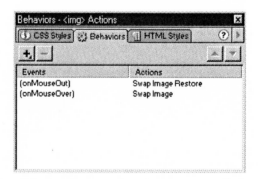

You can add behaviors from Add (+) button and delete the existing behavior with delete (-). A behavior is a combination of an event with an action triggered by that event. The behaviors will be used in chapter 5.

HTML Styles Panel

- To open HTML Styles Panel, choose Window > HTML Styles.

You can create new HTML styles such as Text Bold, Specific Font, Size. You can reapply that formatting to any text in any document using the HTML Styles Panel.

Properties Panel (Property Inspectors)

- To open Properties Panel, choose Window > Properties.

Properties Panel will show properties of a selected object.

Format Properties

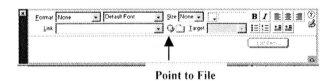

Point to File

The Properties Panel will show the properties of a selected object. You can format a paragraph, the font, size, font color, style, align, and bullet from format properties. If you want to link the text to another document, you can select the text by using the highlight function and clicking the yellow folder to find a document or open the site and moving the pointer from the link (pointing to the file) to a file in site window.

Layer Properties

When you select the layer, layer properties will show details of that selected layer. You can adjust the size, change the name, or change the background or the color of the layer.

Image Properties

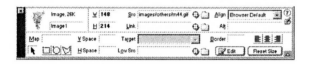

If you select an object, such as an image, the Property Inspector will show you the details of that object. You can assign a name to a selected image, change the size, change the source, link it to a document, align it, place a border, input a statement in Alt field, map images, set target to a blank page or itself. We will learn how to operate them in Chapter 4.

Summary

This chapter is like a reference. You can create a local site and operate the Dreamweaver software from this chapter. You can repeat them at any time while you learn other chapters. You will learn better if you know what tools you have and how they work. I suggest that you not only read this chapter, but also practice operating the Dreamweaver application. In the next chapter, you will start to create your first document, called a home page.

CHAPTER 3
DESIGN

This chapter will help you design your pages. You will learn how to design Web pages using Layout (both Layout Cells and Layout Tables), Tables, Layers, and Frames. You can select the designs that match your requirements and your goals. The Page Layout is a good design tool that can be used with most kinds of page designs. The Table is good for tabular data, or some data that will need to be presented in a table form. Layer used to be popular in Dreamweaver version 3 and is flexible with your own design. Frames are good for multiple pages that show in one frameset. For example, the top frame may contain a logo, a company's name, and a menu, which is static, and the bottom frame may show content, which is dynamic, according to a selected menu.

Design Page Layout

When you have created a local site, you can create documents to put in that site. You can create new documents in Dreamweaver starting from blank pages or templates, if you already have one. I will use the "Taste of Foods" project as an example that you can understand. Later on, you can try to create your own pages.

Document set up and Page Layout

1. Define basic page elements: page title, text color, link color, background color (or background image) and so on
2. Save a document in a local site
3. Design Page Layout
4. Insert images, text, other media (you can modify them any time)
5. Preview in Browser (to check if your document is compatible with the browser and if you need to correct them, you can do at this time)

1. Define basic page elements

- Choose Modify > Page Properties or Move pointer to the working area; click right mouse button > select Page Properties.
- The page properties window appears.

You can set the title of page "Taste of Foods" in the Title field. If you plan to type text (or copy from text file) in page directly, you should set the text color. You can set other available options in this window.

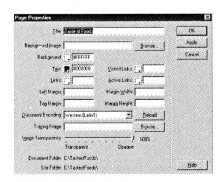

- Click **OK**.

Note: You can type title in the title field on the toolbar and press enter key on keyboard for the page title.

When you finish the page set up, you will see the name "Taste of Foods" shows on the title bar.

Taste of Foods (Untitled-1*) - Dreamweaver

2. Save a document in a local site

- To save a document; choose File > Save (or Save as).
- The "Save As" window appears; Type "**index.html**" in the file name field.
- Click Save button (This file should be in the "TasteofFoods" folder).

You should see the **(Untitled-1*)** on the title bar change to be **(TasteofFoods/index.html)** which showed the site folder (TasteofFoods) and file name (index.html). This file (index.html) will be a home page.

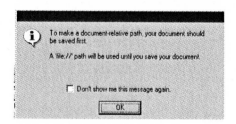

This step (save document for the first time) should be done before insert anything in a document to avoid message "to make a document-relative path, your document should be saved first".

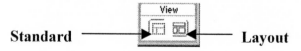

3. Design Page Layout

- To open the Object Panel (actually it is open as default); choose Window > Objects
- Click Layout view from the Object Panel
(You can switch between standard view and layout view)

Standard ———— 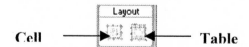 ———— Layout

- Layout Cell and Layout Table will be available to use

Cell ———— Table

Note: If you select standard view, layout cell and layout table will be dimmed (not available) but the layer and table in the Object Panel will be available to use. The layout is designed to substitute the layer and table. If you get used to the layer and table or you want to add layer and table, you can switch between standard view and layout view any time.

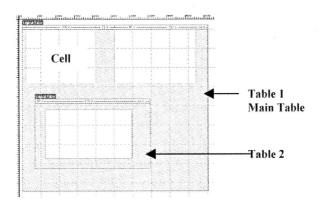

When you insert a layout, you should first insert a layout table (Table 1) before a layout cell. If not, it will create one for you as a container, but the layout cell must be inside the layout table. You can insert many layout cells in a layout table and then insert another layout table (Table 2) in the first layout table (Table 1).

Layout will help you to organize your page. You can resize layout cell and table by click the edge of Table (or cell) and drag table (or cell) to your chosen size. You can move them by point to a table (or cell) with the arrow pointer and drag where you want on the active document.

4. Insert images, text, media objects

- You can add text, images, and media objects to layout cells; click in the cell where you want to insert content, then type text or insert images.

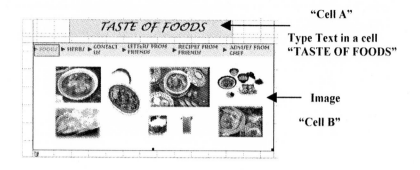

Type Text in a cell
"TASTE OF FOODS"

Image

"Cell B"

This image (menu) created from Fireworks and you can use map tools in Dreamweaver to link to documents (pages).

When you select a cell (Cell A) the layout cell properties will appear, I click the background color (**Bg**) in the properties, the color palette will show and I select light green to be background of that cell.

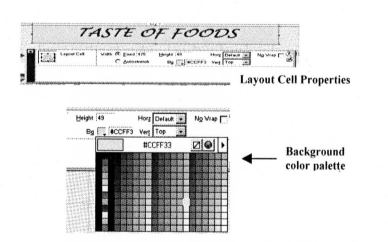

Layout Cell Properties

Background
color palette

Typing "**TASTE OF FOODS**" in a cell and highlight over the text, the format properties will appear. I change font type, size, bold, align center, and font color from the properties. If you want visitor to click this word and link to other page, you can link them via yellow folder.

To insert image to put in Cell B

- Click cell B to make a cell active (cursor will brink in a cell).
- Choose Insert > Image (or click image button in Object Panel).
- The Select Image Source window appears.
- You can select image file from list (in this case, select TASTE.gif).
- Click **Select** button.

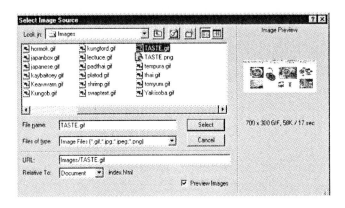

5. Preview in Browser (Internet Explorer, Netscape Navigator)

- To Preview; choose File > Preview in Browser > Internet Explorer (Netscape Navigator) or Press function F12 key on keyboard (it will select the default browser).

64

You should preview in a browser to see if it is compatible with that browser.

Note: Dreamweaver is compatible with Internet Explorer but some features do not work well with the Netscape Navigator such as Table (you can use layer or layout to substitute them), rollover images (you should create the rollover image from fireworks instead and insert as a fireworks HTML). You can find more information from Macromedia (support center) Web site.

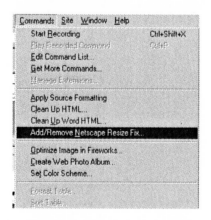

You should Add Netscape Resize Fix... in documents.

- To Add/Remove Netscape Resize Fix...; choose Commands > Add/remove Netscape Resize Fix...

From "Taste of Foods" project, the first page is a home page "index.html"; this page can link to other pages from menu (see picture below). So you have to create pages (Foods.html, Herbs.html, Contact.html, and so on).

To create Foods.html

- Select File > New.
- Follow steps that you create the first page.
- You can type "Foods " in the Title page.
- Save under name "Foods.html" in a "**HTMLFile**" folder that you create from chapter 2.

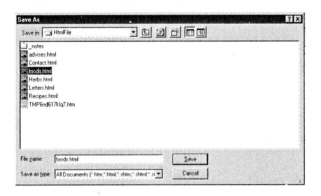

- Click **Save** button.
- The Title bar will show " Foods (HTMLFile/Foods.html)".
- You can insert layout table and layout cells in a document as you desire.

Note: you can create "Herbs.html" and other documents by follow the steps above, change name of document to relate to information of document.   Documents (html files) should be saved in the "**HTMLFile**" folder.

Before we go into the details of other documents (pages), we will link the menu on a home page (index.html) to other documents (Foods.html, Herbs.html, and so on).

We have one image that was created from Fireworks with many images and text, but it shows many words that can be linked to other pages, such as Foods. For instance, when you click on the word "Foods," it should link to the "Foods.html" document. If you click on the word "Herbs," it should link to the "Herbs.html" document, and so on.

You can use map in the properties to map the hotspot (or slice) and link only this part of an image to other document.

To map the hotspot

- Select (click) image in the layout cell
- The image properties will show detail of a selected image.
- Click in the Map field and Type map name "Foodsmap".
- Select the rectangular hotspot tool.

- Drag over a word "FOODS" and release a mouse.
- The hotspot will show over a word "FOODS"

- You can click the yellow folder on the right side of link field.
- The Select File window appears.
- Select (Double click) "HTMLFile" Folder to open.

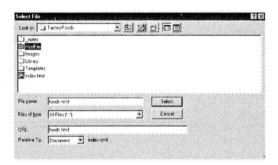

- Select a related document ("Foods.html" file).

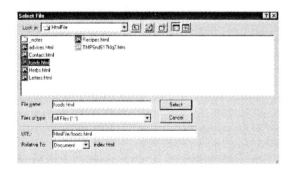

- Click **Select** button.

You can type specific alternative text (**Alt**) that will appear in place of the image for text-only browsers or for browsers that have been set to download images manually. For visually impaired users who use speech synthesizers with text-only browsers, the text is spoken out loud. In some browsers, this text also appears when the pointer is over the image. You can set the target (from properties inspector) to a blank page or over the previous page.

You can preview in browser to see your set up (you should save your document before preview).

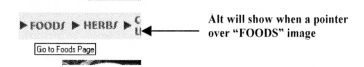

Alt will show when a pointer over "FOODS" image

Note: you can use the visual link on the left side of yellow folder by dragging it to a file in the site window directly. You will see in the link field wills show a linked file.

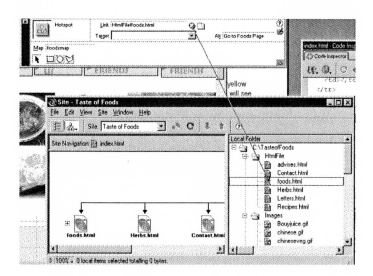

When you have linked documents together, you will see a site map diagram on the left side of site window shows an automatic link.

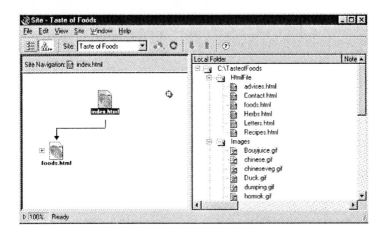

You can create documents (Herbs.html, Contact.html, and so on) for your practice using the steps above to map hotspot in main page (index.html) and link to the related documents. Your site map diagram should look like diagram below after you have created and linked them.

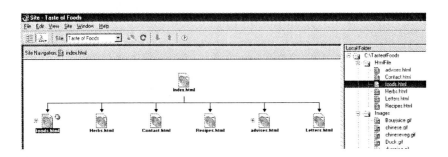

Design Tables

Tables are tools for laying out data and images on an HTML page. You can add a vertical and horizontal structure to a page.

Tables consist of three basic components:
- Row (horizontal spacing)
- Columns (vertical spacing)
- Cells (the container created when a row and column intersect)

To Insert Table

- Change the view from Layout view to standard view in Object Panel.
- Click insert table button (or choose Insert > Table from menu).
- Insert table dialog box appears.

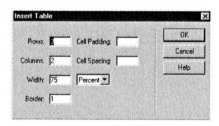

- Insert number of rows and column that you desire in a rows field and columns field.
- Click **OK**.

- Table will be shown in work area.

Note: If you don't want the line around border, select the table as the above. The table properties inspector will show that you can change border number in a border field to be 0(zero). You can change border color from color palette.

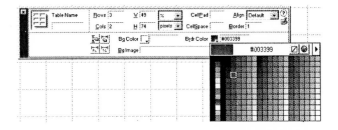

You can also add images or text to table cells. If you want to add text, you can click in a cell and type the text in that cell. You can adjust the font style and color by highlighting the text and changing each property from the Properties Inspector. If you want to insert an image, you can click in a cell and insert an image in that table cell.

To select the entire Table

- Click border of the table.
- The selection handles appear around the table when it is selected.
- You can adjust the entire table by using pointer point to the right or bottom edge and move them.

To select rows or columns

- Position the insertion point at the left margin of a row or Position the insertion point at the top of a column.
- Click when the selection arrow appears.

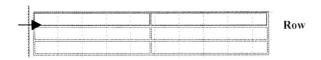
Row

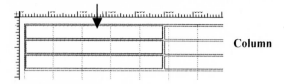

Column

To select cells

- Click in a cell, and drag down or across to another cell.

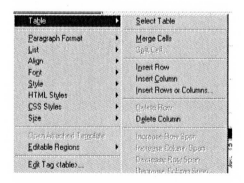

To insert row or column

- Select Row (Left side of table) or Column (Top of table) from table where you want to insert.
- Choose Modify > Table.
- Select Insert Row or Insert Column (depends on what you select before).

Table	▶	Select Table
Paragraph Format	▶	Merge Cells
List	▶	Split Cell
Align	▶	
Font	▶	Insert Row
Style	▶	Insert Column
HTML Styles	▶	Insert Rows or Columns...
CSS Styles	▶	
Size	▶	Delete Row
		Delete Column
Open Attached Template		Increase Row Span
Editable Regions	▶	Increase Column Span
		Decrease Row Span
Edit Tag <table>...		Decrease Column Span

Note: You can delete row or column by use the same menu above but change from insert to be deleted. If you select column at that time, the delete column will show (or if you select row at that time, the delete row will show.

You can split or merge cells by using the Property Inspector with the commands in the Modify > Table submenu to split or merge cells. You can merge any number of adjacent cells (entire selection is rectangular) to produce a single cell that spans several columns or rows (see the sample below).
I am using table to layout the "Foods.html" page. I will create two tables.

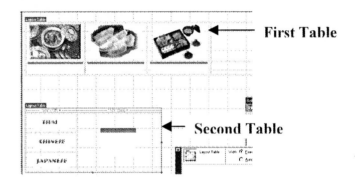

First Table will show the swap image in a table of each Food image.

- Insert images on the first row (First image for Thai Food, Second image for Chinese Food, The third image for Japanese Food).
- Insert swap text image (of each individual image) in the second row (I used the same image that have a line to remark them first but when the pointer point to first image the second row, first column will show Thai (image that create from fireworks), if pointer point to second image in the first row, the second row and second column will show Chinese).

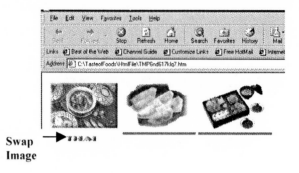

Swap
Image

Preview in Browser:
When pointer point to the image the swap image will appear

Second Table will have images (text) that is shown in rows. If you pointer points to that image in a row, the swap image on the right (or second column) will change according to the image of each row. I merge the second column from 3 rows to be one and use only one swap image for 3 kinds of food.

Merge Cells

- Select adjacent row (the second column).
- Choose Modify >Table.
- Select merge cells.

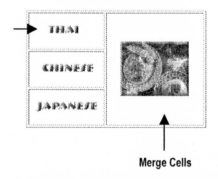

Merge Cells

When pointer point to **THAI** on the first cell (first row, first column), image on the second column change to Thai food.

When pointer point to **CHINESE** on the second cell (second row, first column), image on the second column change to Chinese food.

75

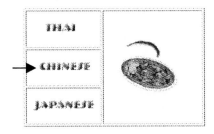

Note: we will discuss on the swap image in chapter 5.

Design Layer

You can create layers on your page easily in order to hold all of your page elements. You can draw a layer on the page, insert a layer through the menu, or drag it onto your page.

To create a layer

- Select layer button in the Object Panel (if it is unavailable, click the standard view in the Object Panel before and the layer button will be available).
- Drag and draw the rectangular in the work area.

If you want to draw more that one layer at this time, you need to hold the Ctrl (control) key on keyboard and the pointer will be shown as a plus (+) sign that you can drag a pointer to draw layers as long as you still hold that Ctrl key.

- You can resize width and height of the layer. When you select that layer, you will see the resize handles and mark around the layer. If you point mouse to any mark (dot) on the handle you can move them left, right, top, or bottom.

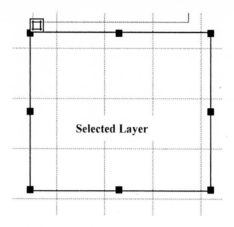

Selected Layer

- You can also create a layer within another layer (nest), put layers on top of each other (stacking), or hide certain layers while showing others.

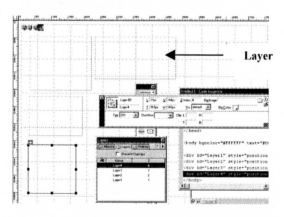

Layer

Layers Panel will list all layers that you create in a document. You can rearrange layer in a list. You can use the Layers Panel to prevent overlaps, to change the visibility of layers, to nest or stack layers, and to select one or more layers.

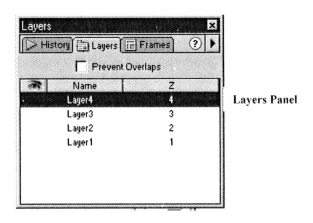

Layers Panel

Layer Properties Panel can be used to specify the name and location of a layer as well as to set other layer options.

Layer Properties Panel

Note: when you insert layers into your page, Dreamweaver inserts the HTML tag for those layers in your code. You can set four different tags for your layers: **div, span, layer**, and **ilayer**. Div and span are the most common tags and are recommended for use so that the widest audience will be able to view your layers. Both Internet Explorer 4.0 and Netscape Navigator 4.0 support layers created using the div and span tags. Only Navigator 4.0 versions support layers created with the layer and ilayer tags (Netscape discontinued support in later browsers). Earlier versions of both browsers display the contents of a layer but do not display the positioning.

Snapping layers to the grid

Use the grid as a visual guide for positioning or resizing layers in the Document window. You can turn this grid on for a guide while you draw your layers. You can also have your layers automatically snap to the grid, and change the grid or control the snapping behavior by specifying grid settings. Snapping works regardless of whether or not the grid is visible.

To display grid and snap a layer

- Choose View > Grid > Show Grid.
- Choose View > Grid > Snap To Grid to turn snapping on (or to turn it off).
- Select a layer and drag it.
- The layer will jump to the nearest snapping position.

Design Frames

Frames can be used for dividing a Web page to multiple pages. You can design a top frame, a side (left or right) frame, and a bottom frame. The most common use of frames is for navigation. A Web page can use one frame to hold the Navigation Menu and another frame to hold the page content. Since the Navigation Menu is in a frame, a visitor to your site can click a menu item and the content will appear in the content frame, but the Navigation Menu will not change at all. This can keep the user oriented within your site.

3 frames
(Top, left, right)

Top (Logo & Company 's name

Left
(Menu)

Right
(content)

To insert a predefined frameset

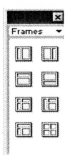

The predefined frameset icons in the Frames category of the Objects Panel provide a visual representation of each frameset as applied to a selected document. You can insert a frameset at any time during your design, but my suggestion is to do them with a blank document when you start to design that particular page, so it will not confuse your design later.

- Click in a document (work area) to place the insertion point in it.
- Select Frames from category of the objects Panel.
- The frameset icons will appear.
- Select a style of frameset.
- Drag an icon directly to a document or click at the document.
- The frameset's style that you select will be inserted in a document (they will be divided by lines for each frame).

Note: You can insert each frame separately or frameset using menu.

- Choose Insert > Frames > left, right, top, bottom, left and top, left top, or split

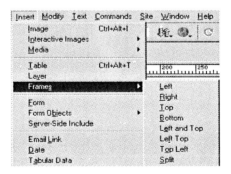

When you insert a frameset to a document, you can modify and adjust the border of each frame. You will need to use the visual aids from the View Menu to show all borders that you can move (left, right, top, or bottom), depending on vertical or horizontal line.

To view frame borders in a document

- Choose View > Visual Aids >Frame Borders.

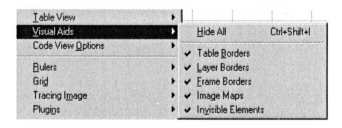

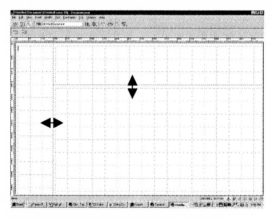

To delete a frame

- Drag the frame border off the page

Frames Panel will show a visual representation of frames within a document.

- Choose Window > Frames (to display the frames

Panel) or Press **Ctrl** + **F10** key on keyboard

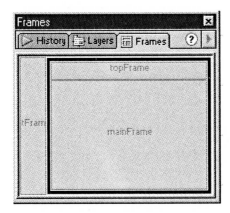

You can click to select each frame from frames Panel.

Save Frame and Frameset Files

You have to save all Frames and Framesets before you can preview the document in a browser. The Frameset file will be a file that shows their relationship. Each frame will still need to be saved individually. Dreamweaver will give a temporary file name, such as "UntitledFrameset-1" for the frameset page. If this is the first page, you should give the name of "index.html." "Untitled-Frame-1," "UntitledFrame-2," and so on for frame pages, and "Untitled-1" for a document.

Save All Files in a frameset

- Choose File > Save All Frames.

This will save all open documents and frameset document.

If this frameset, frames, and documents is saved for the first time.
You will see the "Save As" window display and you can type file
name in the file name field.

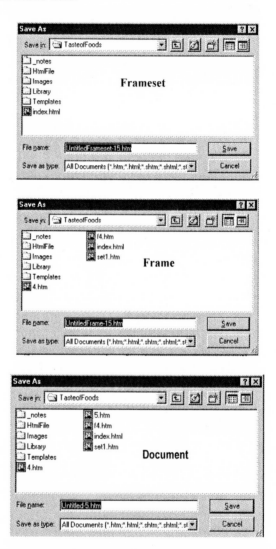

Note: Each of these frames is an independent HTML page. When
you save them, you have to give name to every frame that you
create. They all work together on the page through the use of one

or more framesets.

For example: I create four frames that consist of Corner frame, Top frame, Left frame, and Main frame.

- Corner frame show Logo of a company (static)
- Top frame show Company's name and address (static)
- Left frame show menu (navigation to all pages) (static)
- Main frame show content of pages that will be change when visitor select different topic on menu (Dynamic)

From this example, you can have 3 frames static but one frame must be dynamic when selection change the page will be changed to related content.

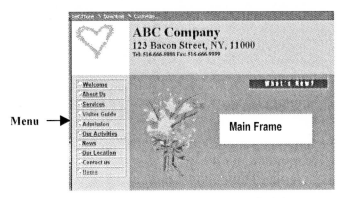

Select Our Location from Menu on the left frame; the main frame is changed content

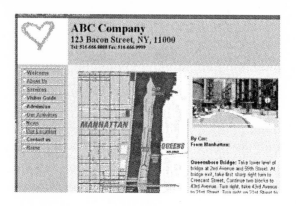

Summary

There are many design tools in this chapter for you to choose from. You don't have to use them all. In previous versions of Dreamweaver, they didn't have the Layout Cells and the Layout Table. Layers can be adjusted any way you want. It also means that you can control your own page. Tables are difficult to use for inserting and adjusting images, but they are good for data tables. You will get used to the Layout Tables and Layout Cells in Dreamweaver 4, because you can manage your page precisely.

CHAPTER 4
MANAGE AND INSERT OBJECTS

You will learn how to manage objects, assets, properties, and behaviors in your design layouts (Layout Cells and Layout Table), layers, tables, or frames. This is a development phase that allows you to insert objects, such as images, texts, buttons, and other medias.

Assets

Assets are elements (Images, Colors, URLs, Flash, Shockwave, Movies, Scripts, Templates, and Library). They are collected in the selected site. After you design a layout in a page, you must gather the assets that you want to use for your pages. They should be ready by the time that you want to develop your site. Your assets can be objects, such as images that you copy from clip-art or that you created in Fireworks. They must be gathered in a folder that you have in a site. From the "Taste of Foods" site, we have already created an "Images" folder. You will need to collect images to put in your "Images" folder. (You can review how to create folders in Chapter 1.) If the Assets Panel does not show on the screen; choose Window > Assets.

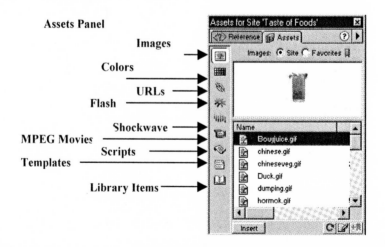

Assets Panel

Images

Colors

URLs

Flash

Shockwave

MPEG Movies

Scripts

Templates

Library Items

- Click Images icon in Assets Panel to see all images in a specific site.
- You will see image preview (selected image from list) and image lists.

Note: You can click other icons to see assets that you collect in the site.

To insert assets

- Click in design view to place the insertion point such as in a layout cell, layer, or table cell
- Select image (or other assets) from list in the Assets Panel (blue highlight will appear on the selected image file and image will show in preview)
- Click "Insert" button on the bottom left of Assets Panel
- Image will appear in the document or you can select the image from a list in the Assets Panel and drag it into the design view where you want it to be appeared.

Insert Image directly to a document (work area) in design view

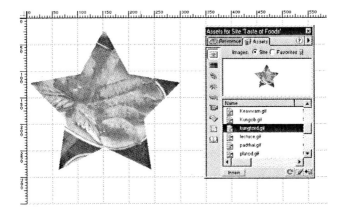

Insert images to a layout cells in design view
(You cannot insert any objects in layout tables without cell)

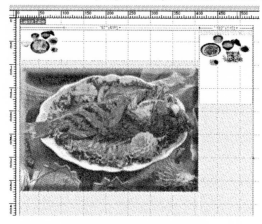

You may have a lot of images and other assets in your site. You can manage them by using Favorite Asset to group them in the related category and giving a name, called a nickname, to each favorite folder.

To add assets to your favorites list

- Select one or more assets from list in Assets Panel.
- Click "Add to Favorites" button on the right side of the Assets Panel.

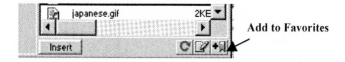

Add to Favorites

Selected assets will be copied to favorites list. You can change from site window (in Asset Panel) to Favorites window.

- Click the option Favorites from the Assets Panel.
- The favorites list will appear.

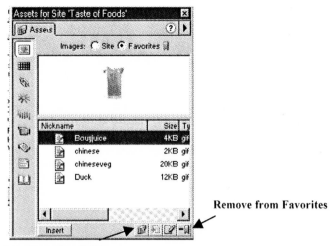

Remove from Favorites

New Favorites Folder

Remove assets from your favorites list

- Select assets that you want to remove
- Click Remove from Favorites button

Note: The assets are removed from the Favorites list, but they still appear in the Site List.

Create Folder (Nickname) for a favorite asset

- Click New Favorites Folder button.
- The folder will appear in a list with untitled name that you can type new nickname for a folder.
- Press enter Key on the keyboard.

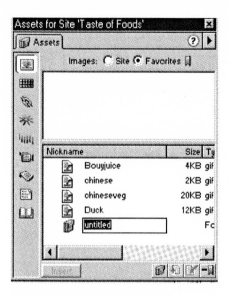

Add favorites asset in a folder

- Drag one or more assets from a list into the folder that you create.

Text

You can type text directly into a document or copy it from another application. It will be processed like a standard word processor. However, it will be better for you to organize and arrange them in layout cells. You can format the text the same way that you type it in the work area, but it is also flexible enough for to move them around a document.

Text can be formatted from Text menu, Properties Panel, HTML Style Panel, or CSS Style Panel.

Format text

- Select text (with highlight).

- Choose Text > Font > select font that you want to change from submenu.

- You can edit font list for the new combination on a list by selecting the Edit Font list.
- The Edit Font List window appears.
- You can select from available fonts.
- Click << button to add in a chosen fonts (you can add more than one font).
- If you want a new fonts in a list, you must click + button (you can delete from a list using – button), then you will have new line to add a new font to the list.

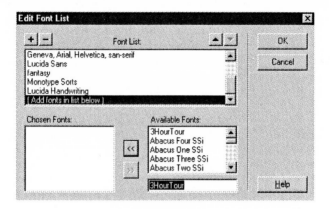

- Choose Text > Style > select style (bold, italic, underline and so on) as your desire.

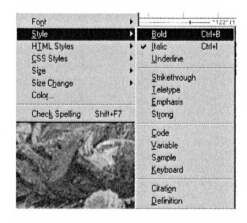

- Choose Text > Size > select size from submenu.

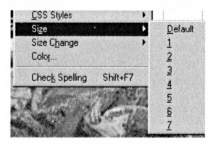

- To increase or decrease the size of selected text, choose a relative size (+ for increase or – for decrease) from Size Change submenu.

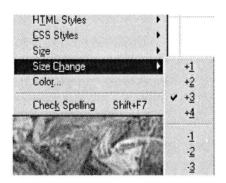

Images

There are three graphic file formats (GIF, JPEG, and PNG) being used in Web pages. Most browsers support GIF and JPEG right now. You should prepare your graphic file in these two formats: GIF and JPEG.

GIF (Graphic Interchange Format) files use a maximum of 256 colors. GIF files are small in size and are best for Web pages. Your pages will load faster with this kind of image. However, graphic color will be dropped.

JPEG (Joint Photographic Experts Group) files can contain millions of colors. The quality of the image will be better than GIF or PNG files. However, the size of JPEG files will be larger than GIF and PNG files, but you can compress JPEG files. Certainly, the download time of JPEG files will be longer than GIF and PNG files.

PNG (Portable Network Group) files are the native file format of Macromedia Fireworks. You can edit PNG files in Macromedia Fireworks and you can export them to be used with other applications, such as with GIF, JPEG, and HTML files.

To insert an image

You can insert images directly into a document, layout cells, layer, table, or frames.

- Click to place the insertion point where you want the image to appear in the document window.
- Choose Insert > Image, or Click the image button on the common category of the Objects Panel.
- The Select Image Source window appears.

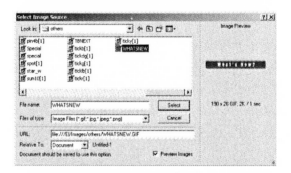

- Browse to select image file from subfolder in the site.
- Click file that you desire.
- Click **Select** button (return to document window).

Set Image Properties in the Properties Inspector

- Select image in the document window.
- Choose Window > Properties inspector.

- To see all properties, click the expander arrow in the lower right corner.

Text Field

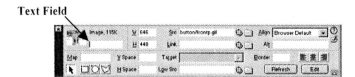

Text Field can be used for the name of image that you can refer to when you are using it with the behavior such as swap image or when you use a scripting language such as JavaScript or VBScript.

W and H reserve space for an image on a page as it loads in a browser. When you insert image, it will automatic reserve the actual size of image but if you set W and H values that do not correspond to the actual width and height of the image, your image may not display properly in a browser.

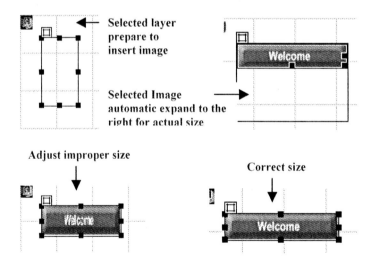

Selected layer prepare to insert image

Selected Image automatic expand to the right for actual size

Adjust improper size

Correct size

Link specifies a hyperlink for the image. You can use yellow folder to browse for a file in your site or drag Point-to-File icon to a file in the Site window. To type manually the URL path can be perform but typing mistake can cause your time to correct them.

Align is to adjust image position. If you insert only one image in layout cell, layer, or table cell, the align will not look very important. You can adjust the way you want and move them around. If you insert image with other element in the same paragraph, line, layout cell, and so on, you can select align from pull-down menu list (Browse Default, Baseline, Top, Middle, Bottom, TextTop, Absolute Middle, Absolute Bottom, Left, Right) to set the horizontal alignment of an image.

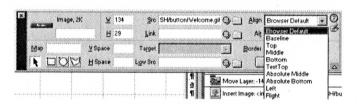

Alt will show text that you type them in a field when the pointer over the image in browsers. You can use Alt as the description of images such as navigation, link to home page and so on. It can be used with the speech synthesizers with text-only browsers; the text is spoken out loud.

Alt: text that shows in browser when move pointer over image (Welcome button)

Map Name Field is used to remark as hotspots. You can divide region in an image using hotspots. It enables you to create client-side image maps. For example, the document contains the image that cannot rollover but it can link to another document when visitors click on hotspots that you map them.

To create an image map

-   Select the image
-   Type a unique name in the Map Name Field

Map Name Field

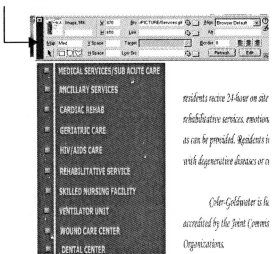

- Select Hotspot tools (Rectangular, Circle, or Polygon) in the properties inspector

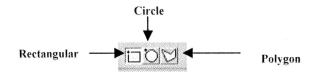

Circle

Rectangular ————► Polygon

- Drag the pointer over the part of image to create a rectangular hotspot
- The hotspot will show and the hotspot properties inspector appear

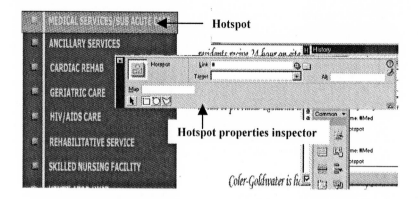

Hotspot

Hotspot properties inspector

- You can browse from yellow folder to find a specific file that you already create for this link. Or you can use the point-to-file icon link to a document in the site window. (You already learn how to link using the point-to-file icon from chapter 2).

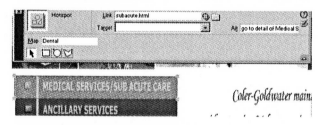

- You can set target to the reserve target name in a pull down list (blank, parent, self, or top).
- Set Alt to specify alternative text that will be display when the pointer moves over that hotspot.

When the pointer move over hotspot in browser

To move a hotspot

- Select the hotspot you want to move.
- Drag that hotspot to new location that you want.

To remove a hotspot

- Select the hotspot you want to remove.
- Press Delete key on keyboard.

Rollover Image

A rollover is an image that changes when the pointer moves over it. You must have two images with the same size for the rollover.

- Primary image display when page first load.
- The rollover image display when the pointer move over the primary image.

To create rollover image

- Choose Insert > Rollover Image.
- The Insert Rollover Image window appear.

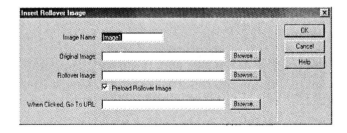

- Type name for the image in Image Name field.
- Browse to insert image for the original.
- Browse to insert the Rollover image.
- Browse for the linked page.

- Click **OK**.

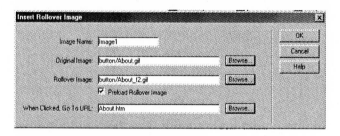

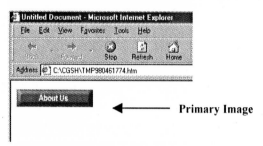

Primary Image

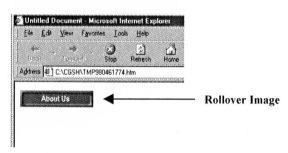

Rollover Image

Media

You can insert media objects such as Flash, Shockwave, MP3 audio, Java applet, QuickTime, ActiveX control, other audio, or video objects into your pages.

To insert media objects

- Click to place the insertion point where you want to insert the object

- Click to select the appropriate button (media objects such as Flash, Shockwave, ActiveX, Plugin, or Applet) from objects Panel

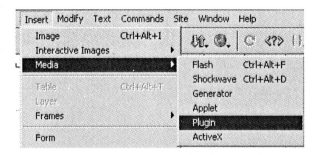

- Select file window appears.
- Select media file that match your selection.

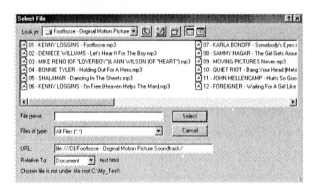

Note: you should prepare media files that you want to use in your site since we start to gather all data to put in a site.

- Click **Select** button.

You can insert a set of designed Flash buttons that Macromedia Dreamweaver provided.

- Choose Insert > Interactive Images > Flash button.

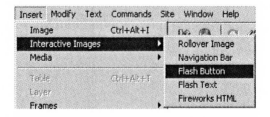

- The insert Flash Button dialog box appears.

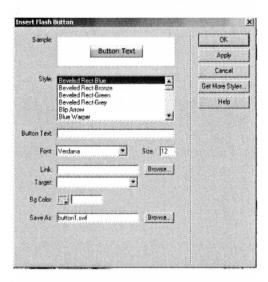

- Select the button style you want from the style list.
- You can type text you want to appear in the Button Text field.
- Select font from the pull-down menu.
- Browse file that you want to link with this button.
- Set Background color in Bg Color field.
- Save as new file name that you want in the same directory as the current document to maintain document-relative links.
- Click **OK** to insert the Flash button in the document window.

You can create and insert a Flash movie that contains just text from the Flash text object. You can use as a text button that you can rollover and link to another page.

- Choose Insert > Interactive Images > Flash Text.
- Insert Flash Text window appears.

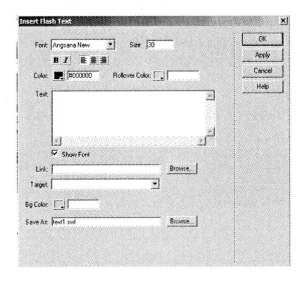

- Select a font from the Font pull-down menu.
- Enter font size in a size field.
- Select style (Bold or Italic).
- Alignment (Left, Center, Right, Justify).
- Select color and rollover color from color palette.
- Type text in the Text field.
- Browse to a file that you want to link.
- You can specify a target for the linked page.
- Choose background color from the Bg Color palette.
- Enter file name in the Save As field (you must save file in the same directory as the current document to maintain document-relative links.
- Click Apply or **OK** to insert the Flash text in the Document window.

Note: You should preview to test your insertion. You can correct them immediately if it is not working well. (Press F12 to preview with default browser)

Named Anchor

You can link to a particular section of a document by creating a named anchor. Named anchor is a marker in documents that will be placed at a specific topic or at the top of documents. First, you must create a named anchor. Second, you must create a link to the named anchor.

To create a Named Anchor

- Click to place the insertion point where you want to create the named anchor.
- Choose Insert > Invisible Tags > Named Anchor.

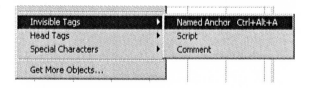

- The Insert Named Anchor dialog box appears.

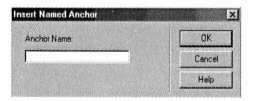

- Type a name for the anchor in the Anchor Name field.
- Click **OK**.

To link to a named anchor

- Select text or image to create a link.
- Type (#) sign and named anchor (case sensitive) in the link field.

From the example, you cannot see everything in the service page but you can see the buttons that you can select to other sections in a page.

The Ancillary Service button in the Service page is set to link to the anchor which is the section that has details of the Ancillary Service. When you click the Ancillary Service button, a section of ancillary service detail will show in the browser.

Create Named Anchor
At this point and give a
named anchor "Ancillary" ➝

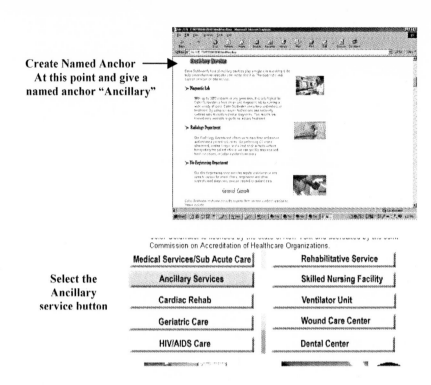

Select the
Ancillary
service button

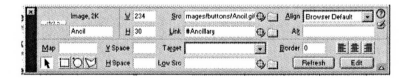

Type #Ancillary in the link
field of Properties inspector

E-mail Link

You can insert a link to specific e-mail address.
- Click to place insertion point in the document where you want to insert e-mail link.
- Choose Insert > E-mail.
- Insert Email Link dialog box appears.

- Type sentence or word in the text field.
- Type e-mail address in the E-mail field.

- Click **OK**.

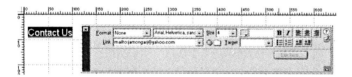

The underline text is linked to e-mail address. You can format text that appears in the document with the format properties inspector. In Link field, Dreamweaver assigns mailto: before the e-mail address.

You can create e-mail link using the format properties inspector.
- Type text in the document.
- Highlight text.
- Type mailto: follow by e-mail address in the link field such as mailto:jamongarj@yahoo.com

Insert Special Characters

- Click to place the insertion point where you want to insert the special character.
- Choose Insert > Special Characters > select from sub menu (Copyright, Register, Trademark, and so on).

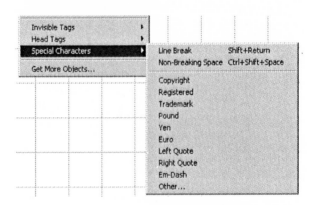

Sample of special characters

You can format them using format properties inspector.

Summary

When you start to develop your pages, you will need to manage your assets to be in the same site. You have to decorate your pages and format them. In this chapter, you learned how to use tools that come with Dreamweaver. Text, images, and media objects must be prepared to insert in the document. They will always involve the Properties Inspector. Objects also use the Properties Inspector for formatting and linking to other pages. For example, you can format text by using the Format Properties Inspector and images by using the Image Properties Inspector. Map (in the properties inspector) is also the useful tool that you can remark as a hotspot and link it to another page. Hotspot can be a part (or spot) of an image that you draw with the rectangular, circle, or polygon to remake them.

CHAPTER 5
BEHAVIORS

Dreamweaver provide various behaviors that you can add to your pages without writing any code or you can call JavaScript from the Behaviors Panel. You can select from Behaviors Panel. A Behavior is a combination of an event and an action. Behaviors are used for interaction on the page such as OnMouseOver (event); the image will be swap (action).

Events are situations that happen while a visitor interacts with your page, such as visitor moving a pointer over a link and then the browser generating an OnMouseOver event for that link. Events must be created before a visitor can interact with the page.

Actions perform specific tasks. Dreamweaver provides a prewritten JavaScript code, such as playing a sound, a pop-up message, or opening a browser window.

Note: You can find additional behavior and actions from Macromedia Exchange Web site and third-party developer site.

To attach a behavior

- Select object such as a button, an image, or a link.
- Choose Window > Behaviors.
- The Behaviors Panel displays.

- Click the Add (+) button.
- Select behavior from the list.

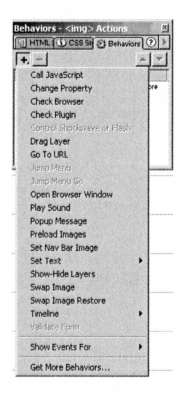

- Enter parameters for the action.
- Click **OK**.

- The default event to trigger the action appears in the events column (You can change event using pop-up menu on the right side of event).

Events in parentheses are available only for links. You can get more behavior from Dreamweaver Web site. When you select Get More Behaviors from menu above, it will link to their Web site (your computer must connect to Internet at that time, otherwise it cannot link to Dreamweaver Web site).

Note: when you learn to create the rollover button from Fireworks, you can export the rollover button to put in Dreamweaver. Behaviors of the rollover button will be attached with the file using HTML extension.

Disjointed Rollover Image

You can swap an image using Rollover image. One image is over another in the same location (images should be the same size). You can see the difference between them when you move your pointer across the browser. The OnMouseOut event will show the original image as an action and OnMouseOver event will show the swap image as an action.

The Disjointed Rollover uses the same concept, but the rollover image will be created at a different location from the original image. The original image will stay the same while you move the pointer over the image, but you will see a second image in the other location at the same time. When we created a table in Chapter 2, you saw the example from the "Taste of Foods" project. There are two tables in a page.

First table show foods. When you move pointer over one kind of food, you will see the name of that food under the picture. Second table show name of foods. When you move pointer over that name (image), the picture will show at the same location on the right side. Concepts of these tables are the same but their styles are different.

To create disjointed rollover

You must have 3 kinds of image to work on disjointed rollover.

1. Original Image shows all the time (onMouseOut and onMouseOver) events.
2. Swap Image is the image that stay when onMouseOut event applies.
3. Second Image is the image that shows when onMouseOver event applies.

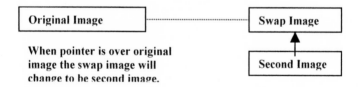

First table

1. Click to select the swap image (This table has the same number of swap images as the original image because we swap them under each original image).

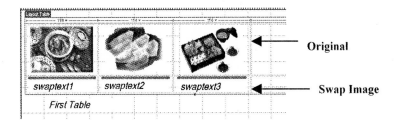

Original

Swap Image

2. In Image Properties Inspector, type "Swaptext1" in a name field (you must give different name to swap image that locate different location).

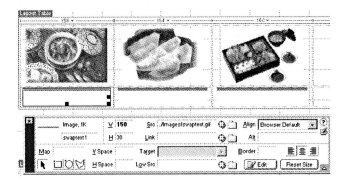

3. Click to select Image (Original image) that you want to create disjointed rollover.

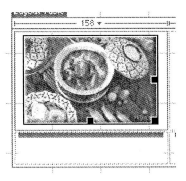

4. In Image Properties Inspector, type name in a name field.

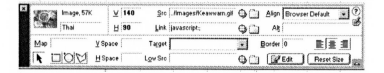

5. Choose Window > Behaviors (if it is not opened on the window).
6. Click Add (+) to open the pull-down menu.
7. Select swap image from menu.

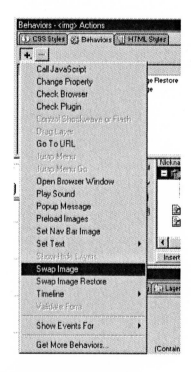

8. The Swap Image window appears.
9. Select "Swaptext1" in images list.

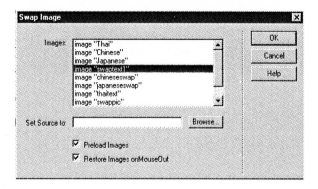

10. Browse to find image (the second image that you what to show when you move pointer over the original image) to put in the "set source to" filed.

11. Select Image Source window appears.

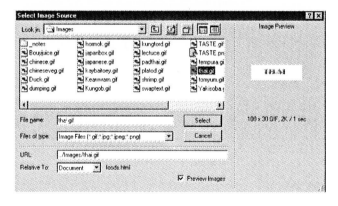

12. Click Select.

13. Return to Swap Image window.

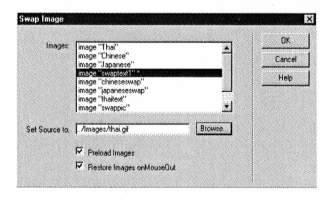

14. Click **OK**.

You can preview in browser to see the swap image.

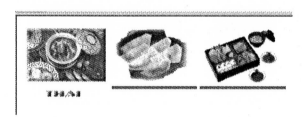

When the pointer is moved over first picture, the image under the picture (Thai) appears.

When the pointer is moved over second picture, the image under the picture (Chinese) appears.

When pointer is moved over third picture, the image under the picture (Japanese) appears.

Note: You can repeat step 1 to 11 for the next disjointed rollover image.

Second Table

1. Click to select the swap image (this table has only one swap image).

Original Image   Swap Image

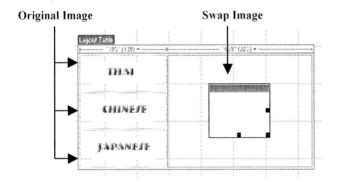

2. In Image Properties Inspector; type "SwapImage" in a name field (The swap image of each Food will show at the same location when you move pointer over each original image.

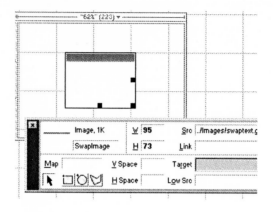

3. Click to select text (original image) that you want to create disjointed rollover.

4. In Image Properties Inspector, type name in a name field.
5. Open Behaviors Panel.
6. Click Add (+) to open the pop-up menu.
7. Select Swap image from menu.
8. The Swap Image window appears

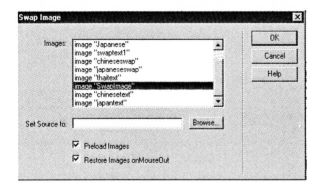

9. Select "SwapImage" in a list.
10. Browse to find image (the second image that you what to show when you move pointer over the original image) to put in the "set source to" filed.
11. The Swap Image Source Window appears.

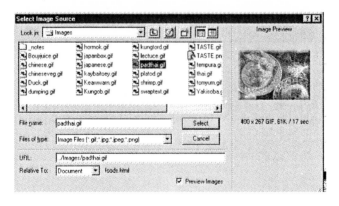

12. Click Select button.
13. Return to Swap Image window.

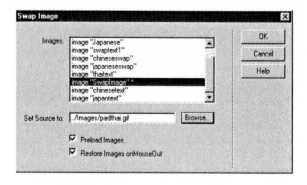

14. Click **OK**.

You can preview in browser to see the swap image.

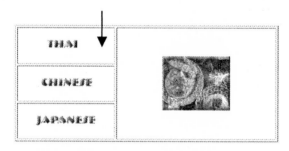

When pointer is moved over the image (Thai), the picture on the right side will appear (Thai food).

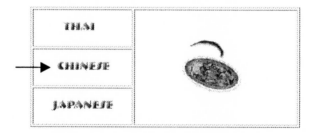

When pointer is moved over the image (Chinese), the picture on the right side will change to be Chinese food.

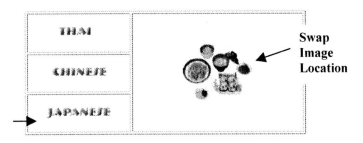

When pointer is moved over the image (Japanese), the picture on the right side will change to be Japanese food.

Note: You can repeat step 3 – 14 for the new images. You can leave step 1 and 2 alone because the Swap Image will show in one location. If the pointer is moved over Chinese (Image), the Swap Image location should show a new food image (Chinese food).

To change a behavior

You can change the event, add or remove actions, and change parameters for actions.

- Select an object that has a behavior attached.
- Open Behavior Panel.

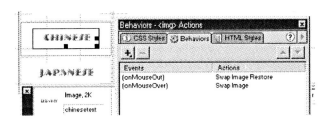

- Double-click the event that you want to change.

124

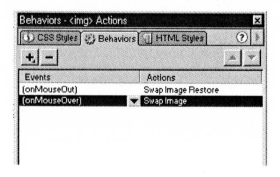

- Change parameters in the dialog box.
- Click **OK.**

To delete a behavior

- Select behavior in the Behavior Panel.
- Click Delete (-) button or press Delete key on keyboard.

Note: there are many behaviors from pop-up menu that you can add to use with the text, buttons, images, and rollover images. You can get more Behaviors from Macromedia Web site, click Add (+) > Get more Behaviors..., this will link to the Web site if you are online at that time.

Test and Publish the Site

Testing is a routine that you have to do regularly, because it allows you to find errors and correct them immediately. While you insert images, links, or media objects, those objects may not be in your local site. You may delete some HTML files or move from one location to the other. This can cause errors. If you test them frequently, you can fix them earlier.

You can test your pages by previewing them in browsers. You should install at least two browsers for your preview because some functions, such as Frames, Rollover, and Table, may not work properly with some browsers. You can adjust them by using substitute functions that work similar to those functions. For example, the Rollover Image function in Dreamweaver may not work properly, but you can create a rollover image from Fireworks and insert the image into a Dreamweaver document.

To preview the document in browsers

- Choose File > Preview in Browser > Select browser (Netscape, Internet Explorer, and so on) or Press F12 (function key on keyboard) to display the current document in the primary browser.

The Check Links feature can be applied to search for broken links in the current document. To do so, you should choose File > Check Links. You can check links in the entire local site by choosing Site > Check Links Sitewide.

When you are ready to publish your site, you will have to copy all related files from your site to the host server. There are many ways that you can transfer your files to the host. If you keep them in local site, you can transfer them all at once using FTP. Many hosts provide formats that you can use for uploading pages. You can set the remote site in the Site Menu.

Before that, you must create local site.

To set remote site

- Choose Site > Define Site.
- The Site Definition window appears.
- Select Remote Info from the category.
- The remote info on the right side displays.
- Select FTP from the Access pop-up menu.
- Enter Host address in the FTP Host field (You have to know the host server address.).
- Enter your host directory (When you register with the host, they should provide you the directory or tell you to create one).
- Enter your login name and password.
- Option to select: **Use Passive FTP** and **Use Firewall.**
- Click **OK**.

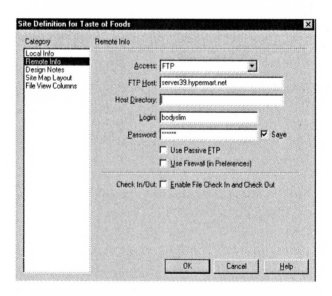

- The Site Window appears.
- Choose Site > Connect.

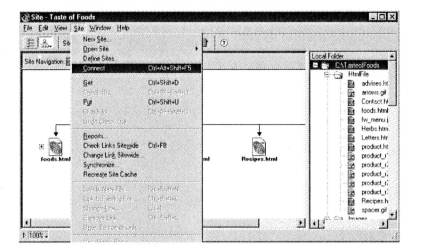

- The Connecting dialog box appears and searching for the host.

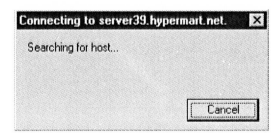

- Choose Site > Put (to transfer files to the server site).
- The Dependent Files dialog box appears.
- Click Yes (To transfer all files in the local site to the server site).

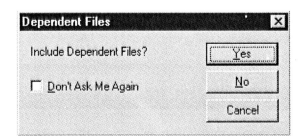

Note: the remote transfer in Dreamweaver may not work properly for all host servers. You can use other FTP applications to do the job.

Summary

Behaviors are the useful functions that can make your Web pages are interesting. You can create swap images, disjointed images, check browser, check Plug-in, and more. While you are working with your Web pages, you should test them frequently to check for errors, links, and browser's compatibility. This way, you can correct them immediately.

CHAPTER 6
FIREWORKS BASICS

This chapter starts with the graphic tools you can use to create Web graphics, such as images, button, text button, and animation graphics. You will learn to familiarize yourself with the menu. Fireworks is a software program that supports Web designers for the creation of Web graphics. You can use Fireworks to create, edit, animate graphics, add advance interactivity, and optimize images in a professional environment. Fireworks combines both bitmap and vector tools.

Macromedia Dreamweaver and Macromedia Fireworks are designed to support each other. You can create or update graphic files in Fireworks and insert or import the files into Dreamweaver. Firework is PNG extension, which is not compatible in every browser yet, but it hopefully will be in the future. You should export and assign a GIF extension or an HTML extension. When you export a Fireworks file, you can export an image only as a GIF file or an HTML file with slice.

System Requirements

For Microsoft Windows

- An Intel Pentium processor (Pentium II or later) running Windows 95, Windows 98, Windows ME, Windows 2000, or Windows NT 4 (with server pack 5)
- RAM 64 MB or more plus 100 MB of available disk space
- 800x600 pixel resolution
- 256 colors display
- CD-ROM Drive
- A Mouse or a Pointer

For the Macintosh

- A Power Macintosh (G3 or higher) running System 8.6 or 9.x
- RAM 64 MB or more plus 100 MB of available disk space
- Adobe Type Manager 4 or later for using Type 1 fonts
- A color monitor (1024x768 resolution)
- CR-ROM Drive
- A Mouse or a Pointer

Macromedia Fireworks provides many resources for learning. You can print the Fireworks manual from the Macromedia Web site, use the Help function in the application, participate in the onscreen interaction lessons, contact the support center from Macromedia Web site, and access several other Web-based information sources.

You have learned how to create pages, design a format for pages, and how to insert graphics, text, and media objects using Macromedia Dreamweaver. Macromedia Fireworks provides graphic tools for creating graphics that you can put into the Dreamweaver. For example, you can create a rollover button in Fireworks and then export it with an HTML file. When you insert that HTML file in Dreamweaver, it will automatically insert it with JavaScript. You don't have to create the rollover again in Dreamweaver. You can preview the page in the browser to see the rollover button.

Vector and Bitmap Graphics

Computers display graphics in vector or bitmap graphic. When you understand the difference between these two formats, you can use them properly and efficiently.

Vector Graphics

Vector graphics describe images using lines and curves,

including color and position information. When you edit a vector graphic, you modify the properties of the lines and curves that describe its shape. You can move, resize, reshape, and change the color of a vector graphic without changing the quality of its appearance. You can also draw and edit a path in Vector Mode. It is a default mode in Fireworks.

Bitmap Graphics

Bitmap graphics describe images using dots (pixels) that are arranged in a grid. You draw and edit pixels in Bitmap Mode. When you select certain tools, it will change to Bitmap Mode. You will see the remark around the border. The title bar will show Bitmap Mode.

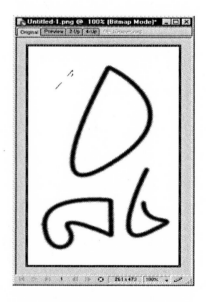

To Open Fireworks Application

- Click Start from Task bar.
- Move pointer to Program menu.
- Find the Fireworks 4.

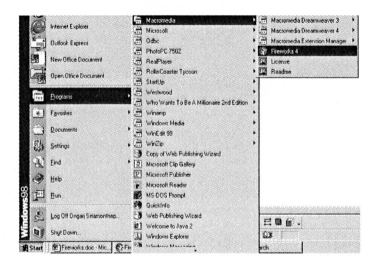

- Click to open program.

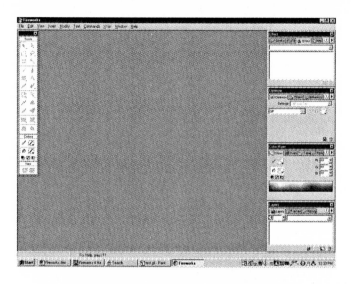

After the Fireworks program is opened, you can select **New Menu** to create a new document or select **Open Menu** to open documents that you have already created from the menu file.

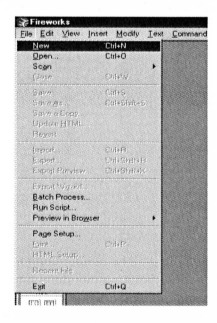

- If you select new menu to create a new document.

- The New Document window appears.

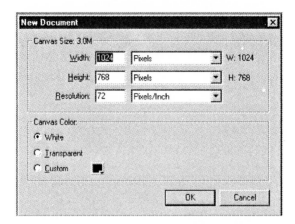

- You can set up canvas size (width, height, and resolution) by typing the number in fields that shows above, and canvas color (white, Transparent, or custom). The default of Canvas Color is white.
- Click **OK**.
- Canvas will appear on the screen with the size that you determined.

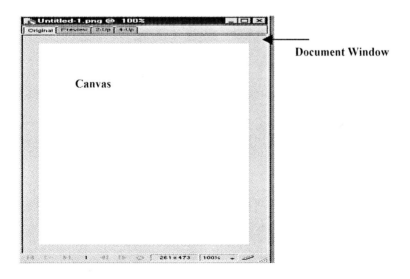

- The document window display tabs (original, Preview, 2-Up, 4-Up).

The Original tab displays the active document that you can create, insert, arrange, and update. The Preview, 2-Up, and 4-Up can be used for previewing export versions of the document.

You can click tab to switch between Original and Previews.

Original

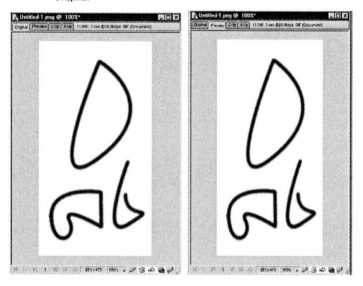

Preview

2-Up

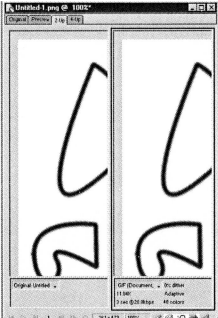

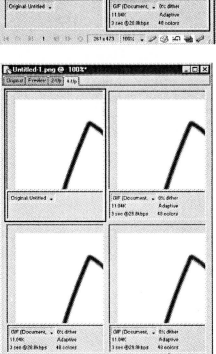

4 - Up

138

In Preview, you can see a graphic as it will be shown in a Web browser. In 2-Up and 4-Up, you can compare optimized versions with the original document.

You can create a new document to be the same size as an existing object.

- Copy an object from the application such as Web objects, another fireworks document, any applications.

- Choose File > New.
- The New document window appears.

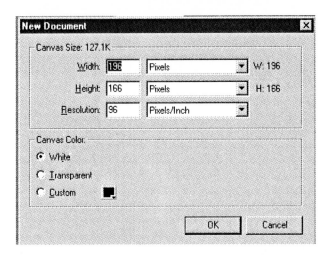

The width and height of canvas show dimensions of the object that you copy.

- Set resolution and canvas color.
- Click **OK**.
- The document canvas appears.

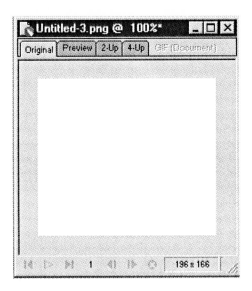

- Choose Edit > Paste.
- The object will fit to the canvas.

To open an existing Document

- Choose File > Open.
- The Open window appears.

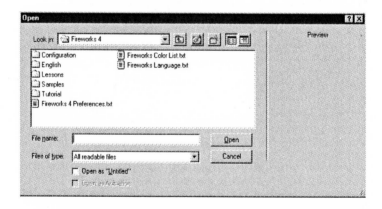

- Select file from the list (or look for the file in the look in field).
- Click **Open** button.

To Save a Fireworks Document

- Choose File > Save.
- The Save As window appears (for the new document) with the temporary filename in a file name field.

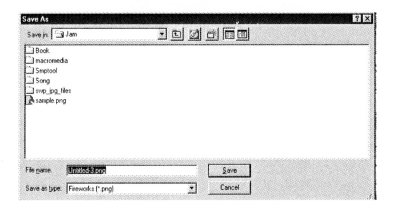

- Type new name in the File name field.
- Click Save.

Note: When a file is created and you choose to save it over the existing file, the file automatically updates without showing the Save As window. You can also Save As another document using the Save As command by choosing File > Save As. The Save As window will appear, so you can give a different name to a file.

Menu

Fireworks consists of menu (File, Edit, View, Insert, Modify, Text, Commands, Xtras, Window, and Help). Each menu will have sub menu that you can choose to work with them.

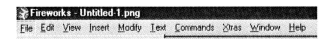

File Menu

New is to create a new document; choose File > New.

Open is to open the exiting document; choose File > Open.

Scan is to import an image from digital camera and scanner. You have to connect camera or scanner to the computer, setup software, and follow instruction. When you scan; choose File > Scan > TWAIN. The imported image is opened as a new document.

Close is to close the active document; choose File > Close

Save is to save the active document. If the document is new, the Save As window appears. You have to give name to a file; choose File > Save. If you update the existing document and click save, the document automatic save a document in the existing name of that document.

Save As can be used when you want to save as a new file; choose File > Save As.

Update HTML updates either Fireworks-generated HTML and images or images only. You can use Launch and Edit from Dreamweaver when updating HTML to preserve the changes you have made to an HTML file that is being edited in Dreamweaver; choose File > Update HTML.

Export can be used when you create such as images, animated images, button, pop-up menu, or rollover images. You can export as an image file, or HTML file (with or without slice); choose File > Export.

Export Preview – Choose File > Export preview.

Export Wizard – Choose File > Export Wizard (It will guide you step by step).

Batch processing is to automatically convert a group of graphic files. You can use batch procession to convert a selection of files to another format, to convert a selection of files to the same format with different optimization settings, to scale exported files, to find and replace text, colors, URLs, fonts, and non-Web216 colors, to rename groups of files by adding a prefix or suffix, and to perform commands on a selection of files; choose File > Batch Process...

Run Script - choose File > Run Script (You must create batch script that you can run script).

Preview in Browser - Choose File > Preview in Browser.

Page Setup – Choose File > Page Set up (To set up the document for exporting, you have to use Modify > Canvas Size or Canvas Color).

Print – Choose File > Print.

HTML Setup can be set a document specific or used as your default setting for all HTML exports. You can change the Document Specific tab to affect the current document only. General and Table settings are global preferences.

Exit is to quit the application; choose File > Exit.

Edit Menu

Edit View Insert Modify Text Commands	
Undo Exit Bitmap Mode	Ctrl+Z
Repeat Exit Bitmap Mode	Ctrl+Y
Cut	Ctrl+X
Copy	Ctrl+C
Copy as Vectors	
Copy HTML Code...	Ctrl+Alt+C
Paste	Ctrl+V
Clear	Backspace
Paste as Mask	
Paste Inside	Ctrl+Shift+V
Paste Attributes	Ctrl+Alt+Shift+V
Select All	Ctrl+A
Select Similar	
Superselect	
Subselect	
Deselect	Ctrl+D
Duplicate	Ctrl+Alt+D
Clone	Ctrl+Shift+D
Find and Replace...	Ctrl+F
Crop Selected Bitmap	
Crop Document	
Preferences...	Ctrl+U
Keyboard Shortcuts...	

Undo and repeat provide in a variety applications.

- Choose Edit > Undo.

- Choose Edit > Repeat.
(You can use History Panel for quick undo and repeat.)

Cut, Copy, and **Paste** are used in every application that runs on window. You can move or edit a selected object using cut, copy or paste.

- Choose Edit > Cut (to remove a selected object from a current position).

Note: Cut means clear when you do not paste before edit the new selected object.

- Choose Edit > Copy (to make a copy of a current selected object).
- Choose Edit > Paste (to paste the cut or copy a selected object).

Copy as Vector can be used to copy selected Fireworks paths to other applications such as FreeHand, Flash, Adobe Photoshop, Illustrator, or CorelDraw.

- Choose Edit > Copy as Vector.

Duplicates of the selection appear in a cascading arrangement from the original; each new duplicate becomes the selected object.

- Choose Edit > Duplicate.

The **clone** of the selection is stacked precisely in front of the original and becomes the selected object. To move a selected clone away from the original with pixel-by-pixel precision, use the arrow keys. This is handy if you want to maintain specific distances between clones or maintain the alignment of the clones.

- Choose Edit > Clone.

Find and Replace can be use to search for and replace element in a document such as Text, URLs, Fonts, or Color.

- Choose Edit > Find and Replace.
- The Find and Replace window appears.

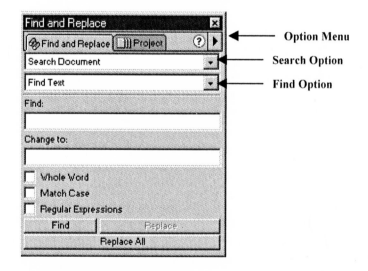

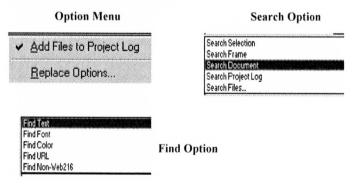

- Select Option from Option Menu.
- Select Search Option from pull-down menu.
- Select Find Option from pull-down menu.
- Type information in a Find field to search for your element.
- Type information that you want to replace in the Change to field.
- Click Replace (one by one) or Replace All.

Preferences

Preference settings control the general appearance of the user interface, edit, and folder aspects.

- Choose Edit > Preferences.
- The Preferences window appears.
- Select the group of preferences you want to modify from tabs.
- Click **OK** after changes.

General Preferences

Undo steps can be set between 0 and 100. It applies to both Undo command and the History Panel.

Color Default sets the default colors for brush strokes, fills, and highlight paths.

Interpolation sets scaling methods and quality. The Bicubic is the sharpest and highest quality and is the default.

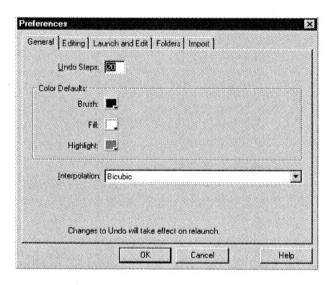

Editing Preference

The Editing Preferences control the pointer appearance and visual cues for working in Bitmap Mode. The check marks are for selecting the options that will provide the editing preferences. The default of this setting shows in a preference window (Editing) below.

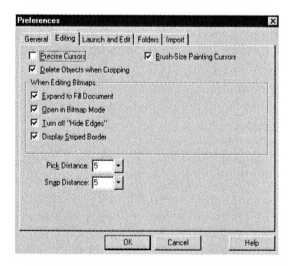

Launch and Edit Preferences

Launch and Edit Preferences control the setting of the Fireworks source files. You can select from the pull-down menu.

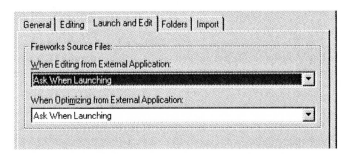

When Editing from External Application and **When Optimizing from External Application** have a pull-down menu with three options. If you want the original Fireworks source (PNG) file will open when you use Fireworks to edit an image or optimize a graphic from within Dreamweaver.

Folders

You can set Folder Preferences to access additional materials (Photoshop plug-ins, texture files, and pattern files) from external sources. You can set Scratch Disks to store temporary cache files.

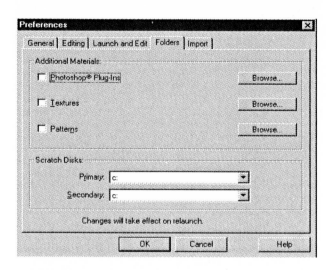

Import

The preference is to set the Photoshop File Conversion when these types of files are imported into Fireworks.

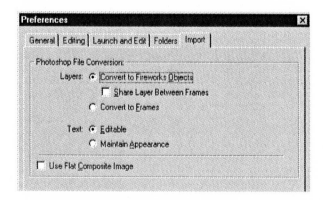

Keyboard Shortcuts is use to access commands, and to choose a tool such as (**Ctrl + S**) is a shortcut of **Save** command, (**Ctrl + V**) is a shortcut for Paste, and so on. You can custom your own shortcut for your convenience.

Note: The standard shortcuts can be used in a variety application,

you should know some of them for fast action such as **New (Ctrl +
N)**, **Open (Ctrl + O)**, **Save (Ctrl + S)**, **Cut (Ctrl +X)**, **Copy (Ctrl
+C)**, **Paste (Ctrl+ V)**, and more.

- Choose Edit > Keyboard Shortcuts.

View Menu

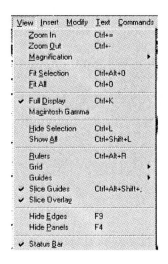

Zoom In, Zoom out, and Magnification

The zoom range (In and Out) in Fireworks is between 6%
and 6400%. If you choose Zoom In or Zoom Out, it will zoom to the
nearest percent, such as the original is 100%. You can select Zoom
In (200%) or Zoom Out (50%). You can also select a specific
percentage from the pull-down menu.

Original at 100%

   -   Choose View > Zoom In.

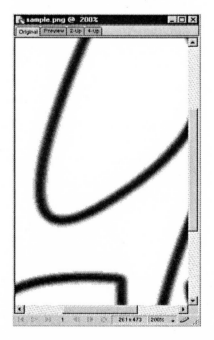

- Choose View > Zoom Out.

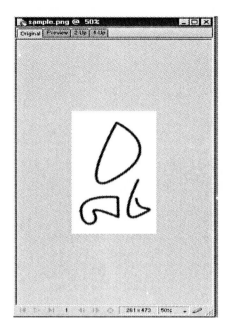

- Choose View > Magnification > Select from list (6% to 6400%).

Note: you can click to select zoom setting from the pull-down menu on the bottom right corner of document window.

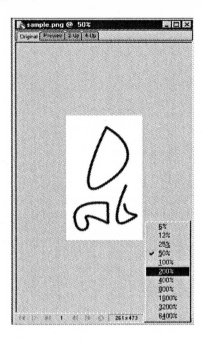

Rulers, Grid, and Guides

You can use Guides and Rulers to layout objects in Fireworks document the way you want or turn on the grid and snap objects to grid.

Rulers

- Choose View > Ruler (to show or to hide rulers)
- Vertical and horizontal rulers appear

Guides

Guides are lines that you drag from the rulers into the document canvas both vertical and horizontal.

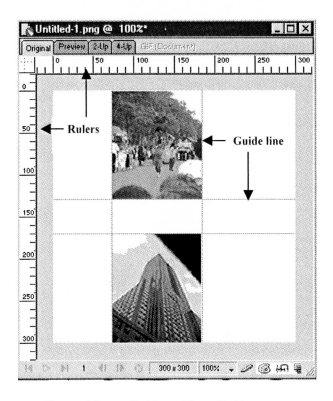

- Choose View > Guide > Show Guides
- Choose View > Guide > Snap to Guides

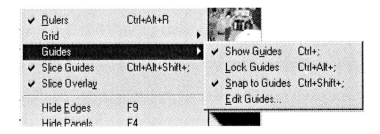

Insert Menu

New Button, New Symbol, and Libraries

You can insert Buttons, symbols, and select to insert from Libraries.

A button is the rollover image that encapsulates up to four different states. Each state represents a button's appearance in response to a pointer action:

1. The **Up** state is the default or at-rest appearance of the button.
2. The **Over** state is the way the button appears in a Web browser when the pointer is moved over it.
3. The **Down** state is the appearance of the button after it has been clicked, typically as displayed on the destination Web page.
4. The **Over While Down** state is the appearance of the Down state button when the pointer is moved over it.

You can create a button with two states (Up and Over) to be used in a Web page. The navigation button may need four states. (Chapter 9, you will learn to create and insert button.)

157

- Choose Insert > New Button.

You can create a symbol from any object, text block, or group.

- Choose Insert > New Symbol.

You can create buttons and save them in Libraries to reuse again in your site.

- Choose Insert > Libraries > Select from pop-up menu.

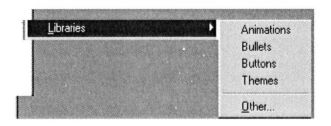

Convert to Symbol

When you draw graphics on canvas, it is a vector object that can be changed or edited at each connection point. When you want to put your graphics in Libraries or animate the objects, you will have to convert them to a symbol. You will not see each connection point on the symbol because it connects as a unit.

- Choose Insert > Convert to Symbol.
- The Symbol Properties window appears.
- Type name in symbol field.
- Select type of symbol (Graphic, Animation, or Button).

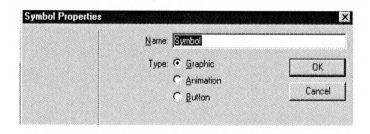

Graphic before convert to symbol   **Graphic after convert to symbol**

Hotspot and Slice

You can use Hotspot and Slice to create interactive objects, such as rollovers and image maps. Hotspots and slices are called Web objects. You can view, select, and rename them through the Web Layer in the Layers Panel.

A hotspot is an area of a Web graphic that links to a URL. An image map is a graphic that will contain several hotspots. Fireworks lets you generate hotspots in virtually any shape (rectangular, circular, polygon) you need, and allows you to export the HTML code to reproduce your image map on the Web.

159

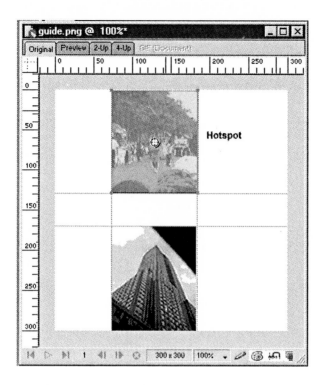

- Choose Insert > Hotspot.

You can use slicing to divide a Fireworks document into different segments and export each segment to a separate file for downloading or to replace part of an image with HTML text. Slice can optimize an image's file size, create interactivity, and swap out parts of an image.

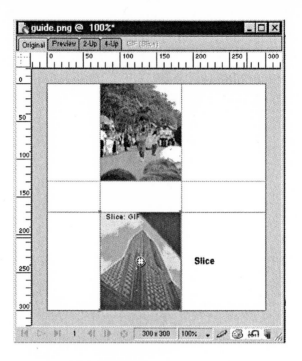

- Choose Insert > Slice.

Pop–up Menu

Pop-up menus are menus that will display a list of submenus when the pointer is the rollover position. A pop-up Menu must be created with slice or hotspot. You can customize the menu by choosing from a selection of font types, cell colors, and background image styles. You can insert a submenu as a table cell. (Detail in Chapter 9)

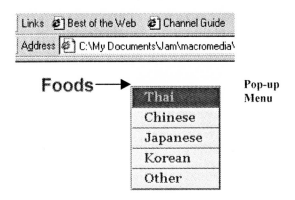

- Choose Insert > Pop-up Menu.

Image

An image can be inserted to a Fireworks document. You can insert more than one image into a document and set the image properties using the available Panels, such as the Stroke Panel, Effect Panel, and Fill Panel.

- Choose Insert > Image.

Empty Bitmap

You can use empty bitmap to create a new bitmap.

To insert an empty bitmap image

- Drag in an empty area in the document with a marquee or lasso tool.
- Choose Insert > Empty Bitmap.

Layer

You can create many layers in one document. Each layer may contain many objects. Fireworks stacks layers based on the created order, placing the most recently created layer on the top of the stack. The stacking order of layers determines how objects on one layer overlap objects on another. You can rearrange the order of layers, as well as the order of objects, within a single layer.

To insert Layer

- Choose Insert > Layer.

Frame

You can create animation-using frames. You can determine the number of frames, give a name to each frame, set a time delay for each frame, and move objects from one frame to another. (See Chapter 11 Animation for details.)

- Choose Insert > Frame

Modify Menu

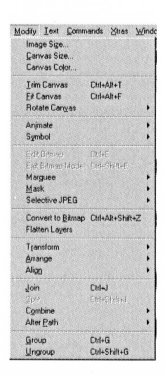

You can modify the size of images, canvas size, and canvas color in an active Fireworks document. The Modify Menu allows you to manage canvas, such as trimming, fixing, and rotating. You can also use Modify Menu to manage objects and symbols in the document such as Animate, Transform, Arrange, Align, Join, Group, and Ungroup.

Image Size

All images in a document and the canvas will be scaled as you type the width and height in the fields.

- Choose Modify > Image Size.
- The Image Size dialog box appears.
- Type numbers (your desired image size) in the width field and Height field.

When you type numbers in the width field, the height field will adjust automatically to balance the canvas size. The images inside the canvas will scale (maximize or minimize depending upon your scale in the width and height field) as the canvas changes. The print size will also be adjusted as the Pixel Dimension changes.

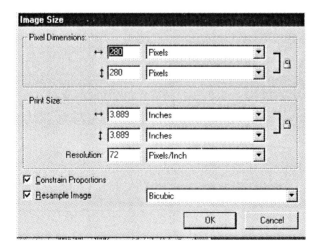

164

Canvas Size

When you modify the canvas size, it will scale upon your adjustments, but the size of the images on the canvas will not change.
- Choose Modify > Canvas Size.
- Canvas Size Dialog box appears.
- Type numbers (your desired canvas size) in the width field and the height field.
- Click **OK**.

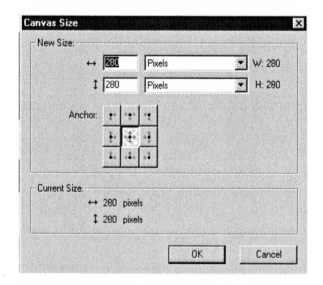

Canvas Color

You can choose three options on Canvas Color.
1. White (Default)
2. Transparent
3. Custom (you can select from color palette on the right side of custom option)

- Choose Modify > Canvas Color.

- Select one option from those three options.

- Click **OK**.

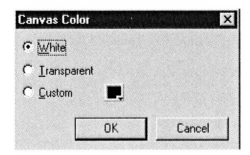

Trim Canvas

You can adjust the canvas to fit your image using the Trim Canvas command. This command can only be used with a canvas that is larger than an image, it will resize to wrap around image.

- Choose Modify > Trim Canvas.

Rotate Canvas

- Choose Modify > Rotate > Select fro submenu.

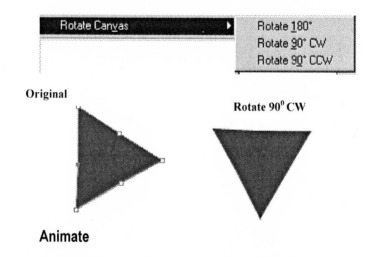

Animate

You can use animate command to convert object to an animation symbol.

- Choose Modify > Animate > Animate Selection.
- The Animate dialog box appears.
- You can set the number of frames, Move, direction, scale to, Opacity, Rotate (CW, CCW).

- Click **OK**.

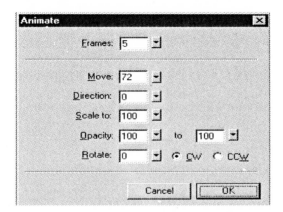

Frames are the number of frames you want to include in the animation. Although the slider only lets you set a maximum of 250, you can use the edit field to type in any number you wish. The default is 5.

Movement is the distance, in pixels, that you want each object to move. Possible values range from 0 to 250 pixels. The default is 72.

Direction is the direction, in degrees, in which you want the object to move. Possible values range from 0 to 360 degrees.

Note: You can also change Movement and Direction values by dragging the object's animation handles.

Scaling is the percent change in size from start to finish.

Possible values range from 0 to 250. The default is 100%.

Opacity is the degree of fading in or out from start to finish.

Possible values range from 0 to 100. The default is 100%.

Rotation is the amount, in degrees, that the symbol rotates from start to finish. Possible values range from 0 to 360 degrees. You can type in higher values for more than one rotation. The default is 0 degrees.

CW and **CCW** are the direction in which the object rotates. CW indicates clockwise and CCW indicates counter-clockwise rotation.

Symbol

You can create animation for a symbol to move from one place to another using the Tween Instance command.

Tweening is a traditional animation term that describes the process in which a lead animator will draw only the key frames and the assistants will draw the frames in between. In Fireworks, tweening blends two or more instances of the same symbol, creating interim instances with interpolated attributes. Tweening is a manual process that is useful for more sophisticated movement of an object across the canvas and for objects whose Live Effects change in each frame of the animation. (Source from Macromedia Fireworks 4 Helps.)

-    Select Two or more symbols from the same libraries to set the position that you want the object to move

Note: You can select three objects by holding the Shift key on keyboard (do not release until you are finish select the last object) and click pointer on the objects that you want (one at a time). You will see the mark around the object (it means selected)

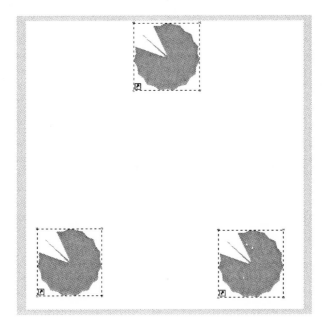

- Choose Modify > Symbol > Tween Instances.

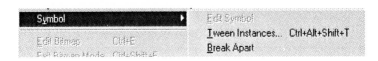

- The Tween Instances dialog box appears.
- Set steps (number of move).
- Click Check mark in a box of Distribute to Frames (Fireworks will generate frames for the movement of objects).
- Click **OK**.

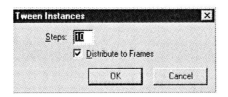

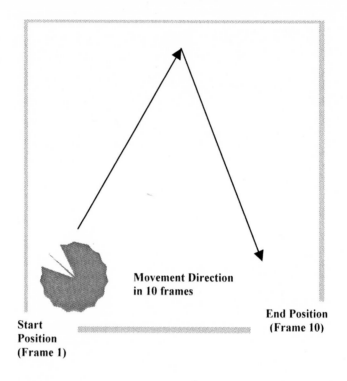

Movement Direction in 10 frames

Start Position (Frame 1)

End Position (Frame 10)

You can use mask techniques to create unique effects by blending the colors in overlapping objects. A mask has two primary uses:

1. The path of a vector mask can outline another object or image. It masks the underlying object or image to its path.
2. A mask object's pixels can affect the visibility of another object. Masks are commonly used to define gradient transparency for other objects.

    - Choose Modify > Mask.

Transform

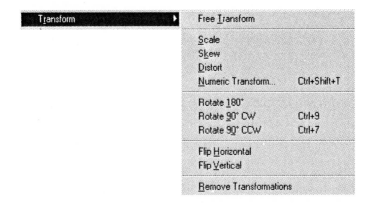

You can scale, skew, distort, and numerically transform your graphics using the Transform Menu and Transform Tools. The Transform Menu also provides the rotation and flip.

- Choose Modify > Transform > Select from pop-up menu.

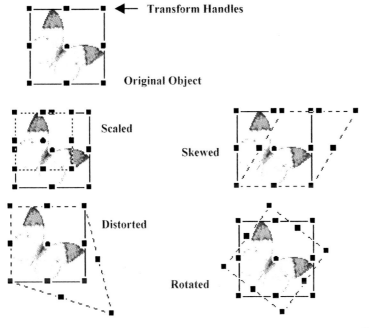

Flipped Vertical

Arrange

The arrange command can be used for overlapping objects. You can send objects to the Back or bring them to the Front.

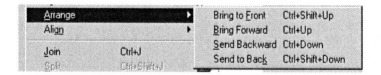

Send the fruit basket to back

Group and Ungroup

You can use group to edit many objects on the canvas as a single unit. If you mcve, transform, or change attributes of the group, all the objects in the group will change. You can ungroup to release them from group and it will be recognized as individual object again.

- Select object that you want to group them; drag pointer over the objects that you want to group

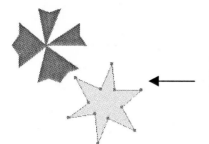

The selected object moves
when you drag pointer to the
new position. Another object
will stay at the same position.

Both objects moves when you
drag pointer to the new
position because they are
selected as a group ——————▶

- Choose Modify > Group.

To ungroup

- Choose Modify > Ungroup.

Text Menu

You can format text from menu.

- Choose Text > select from sub menu (Font type, Size, Style, and align).

Note: You can also use the font icon from Tools box and a text window appears for you to format them in that window. (You will see more detail in chapter 8 create objects, section Tools box and chapter 9 text and button.)

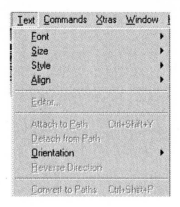

Commands Menu

You can rename or delete commands that appear in the Commands menu.

To rename a command

- Choose Commands > Edit Command List > Select a command.
- Click Rename.
- Enter a new name.
- Click **OK**.

To delete a command from within Fireworks

- Choose Commands > Edit Command List.
- Select a command and click Delete.

Xtras Menu

Filters on the Xtras Menu and in the Live Effects Panel help to improve and enhance the colors in your bitmap images. Fireworks includes many new color adjustment filters. You can adjust the contrast and brightness, the hue and color saturation, and the tonal range.

- Choose Xtras > select from menu (Adjust Color, Blur, Other, Sharpen, or Eye Candy 4000 LE)
- Each menu will have pull-down menu that you can select one command at a time

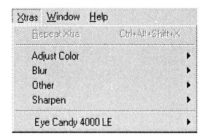

Window Menu

The Window Menu is used to switch opening and closing Panels and toolbars and for creating new window in the Fireworks application. You can click to select them on and off.

Window Help

New Window	Ctrl+Alt+N
Toolbars	▶
✔ Tools	
Stroke	Ctrl+Alt+F4
Fill	Shift+F7
✔ Effect	Alt+F7
Info	Alt+Shift+F12
✔ Optimize	
Object	Alt+F2
Behaviors	Shift+F3
✔ Color Mixer	Shift+F9
Swatches	Ctrl+F9
Color Table	
Tool Options	Ctrl+Alt+O
✔ Layers	F2
Frames	Shift+F2
History	Shift+F10
Styles	Shift+F11
Library	F11
URL	Alt+Shift+F10
Find and Replace	Ctrl+F
Project Log	
Cascade	
Tile Horizontal	
Tile Vertical	
✔ 1 Untitled-1.png @ 100%"	

New Window

You can create multiple views to see one document at different magnifications simultaneously. When you change one view, it automatically appears at different magnifications in different views. This command should be used with the Cascade, Tile Horizontal, or Tile Vertical and helps you to arrange windows.

-   Choose Window > New Window.

177

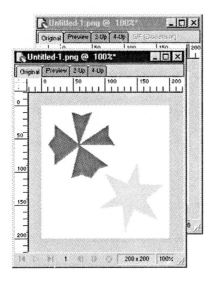

- Choose Window > Cascade, Tile Horizontal or Tile Vertical.

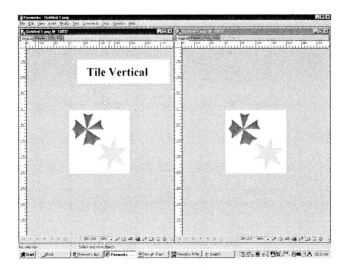

- Select zoom from one window and edit graphics.

To close the window

- Click the close button on the top right corner of the window.

Toolbars

There are Main group and Modify group.

- Choose Window > Toolbars > Main (Modify).

Main   Modify

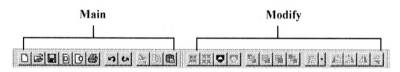

Tools box

Tools, that have triangle on the right corner of icon, show that you can select other options from those tools

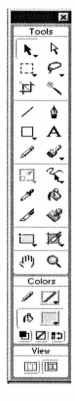

Note: you will learn to operate tools in chapter 8 Create Objects using Tools.

- Choose Window > Tools.
- Tools box (Panel) appears.

Stroke, Fill, Effect and Info Panels

- Choose Window > select Stroke, Fill, Effect, or Info.
- Group Panels appear with the selected Panel on top.

Note: The Group Panels can be switch by clicking the specific tab.

Tab

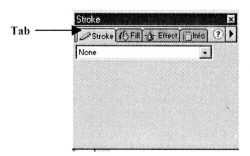

Optimize, Object, Behaviors Panels

- Choose Window > select Optimize, Object, or Behaviors.
- Group Panels appear with the selected Panel on the top.

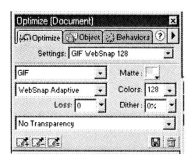

Styles, Library, and URL

- Choose Window > select Styles, Library, or URL.
- Group Panels appear with the selected Panel on the top.

Color Mixer, Swatch, Table, and Option

- Choose Window > select Color Mixer, Swatch, Table, or Option.
- Group Panels appear with the selected Panel on the top.

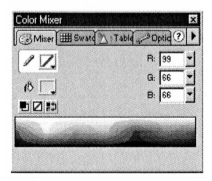

Layers, Frames, and History

- Choose Window > select Layer, Frames, or History
- Group Panels appear with the selected Panel on the top

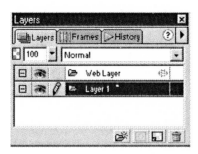

You can view, modify, undo, and repeat multiple actions using the History Panel. You can repeat each step using the replay button. You can also save actions for reuse by using the Save button. (You must first select the command that you want from the History Panel.)

Find and Replace, and Project Log

- Choose Window > select Find and Replace, or Project Log.

- Group Panels appear with the selected Panel on the top.

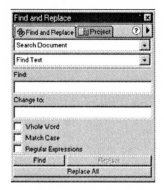

Help Menu

You can access help any time while you are using the Fireworks application.

- Choose Help > select help (Using Fireworks) from menu, what is New, Lessons or link to Fireworks support center at the Dreamweaver Web site.

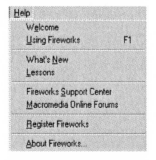

Exercise: The menu on the "Taste of Foods" home page and the images in the middle of menu are created from Fireworks and save as a GIF file.

- Determine canvas size for menu and images.

- Choose Insert > Image, and click to paste image on the canvas (if you want to insert more than one image, you can repeat this step again.)
- Adjust the image size as your desire.
- Select rectangle icon from tools box and drag on the canvas to create the menu.
- Select text icon and click on the rectangle image on canvas.
- Text editor appears, type "Foods".
- Format text and color, and click **OK**.
- Adjust text to fit in the rectangle.
- You can add more text for the Herbs, contact us, and so on and put on the rectangle on canvas.
- Export as a GIF file to put in the local site (site Folder).

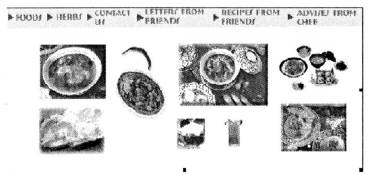

Summary

You have learned how to start the application and save using the Save or Save As command from this chapter. A menu is available in all applications, but they each have some similar and different features that you will have to know before you can use them effectively. The File, Edit, Insert, and Modify Menus are regularly used to create, add, change, update, and save graphics. You can switch Panels on and off from the Window menu. For instance, the Text Menu is for text format. The Command Menu can be used for editing commands in the Fireworks. The Xtras Menu is for changing the features and colors of graphics. You can learn and find more information about these features from the Help Menu.

CHAPTER 7
CREATE OBJECT USING TOOLS

Fireworks has two drawing modes, which are Vector Mode and Bitmap Mode. The Pencil, Brush, and Pen tools can be used to draw freeform vector paths. The Transform Tool (Scale, Screw, Distorted, Rotate, and Flip) and the Drawing Shape Tool (Rectangle, Rounded Rectangle, Circle, and Polygon) are also used with a vector object. The Vector Mode is in default when you start the Fireworks application. If you convert to Bitmap Mode, it cannot be converted back to Vector Mode again. When you select the Bitmap Mode, the rectangle around the border of the canvas appears. Bitmap images are made up of pixels. You can choose many tools from a tools box, such as the Lasso tool, Rubber Stamp, Crop, and Marquee tool.

Tools Box

Tools box consist of:

1. Pointer Tool, Select Behind Tool, and Export Area Tools
    You can switch between these three tools using the triangle at the bottom right corner of the icon. You can use Pointer to select the single object and multiple objects.

2. Subselection tool
    Subselection Tool can be used to select an individual connected point of the object in Vector Mode. In Bitmap Mode, it cannot be use to edit an individual connected point.

3. Marquee and Oval Marquee Tools
4. Lasso and Polygon Lasso Tool s
5. Magic Wand Tool
    Marquee, Lasso, and Magic Wand Tools can be used in Bitmap Mode. After selecting pixels with a marquee

or lasso tool, you can move a marquee border without affecting the pixels beneath it and you can edit the marquee border. You can manually add or delete pixels from a marquee border using modifier keys. You can also expand or contract the marquee border by a specified amount, select an additional area of pixels around the existing marquee, smooth the border of the marquee, or create a floating selection of pixels. A floating selection allows you to edit, move, cut, or copy a selected area of pixels. These tools can be used with the floating images such as pictures from digital camera. (See section Bitmap Object)

6. Crop Tool
   You can use crop tool to eliminate outside selected area of the object.

7. Line Tool
8. Pen Tool
9. Drawing Basic Shape: Rectangle, Rounded Rectangle, Circle, and Polygon Tools
10. Pencil Tool
11. Brush and Redraw Path Tools
    Line, Pen, Draw basic shapes, Pencil, and Brush Tools are used for drawing purpose.

12. Text Tool
    You can design text-using features that are available.

13. Transform Tools (Scale, Screw, Distorted, Rotation)
    You can transform object the way you want using these transform tools.

14. Freeform, Reshape Area, Path Scrubber Additive, and Path Scrubber Subtractive Tools
15. Eye Dropper Tool

16. Paint Bucket Tool
17. Eraser Tool
18. Rubber Stamp Tool
19. Hotspot (Rectangle, Circle, Polygon) Tools
20. Slice and Polygon Slice Tool
21. Hand Tool
22. Zoom Tool
23. Stroke Color Palette
24. Fill Color Palette

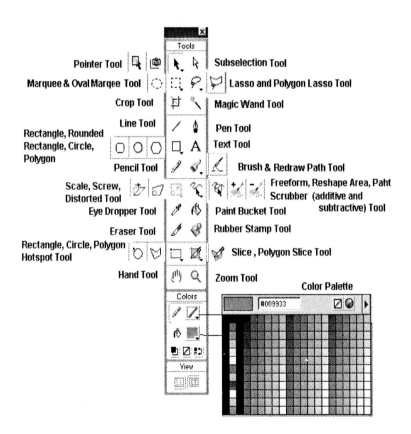

Stroke Panel

Stroke Panel is available with many tools like Drawing Tools (Pen, Pencil, Brush, Drawing basic shapes, and line) and Text.

Stroke Panel consists of:

- Type of stroke such as Pencil, Basic, Air brush and more (you can select to match the tools that you are using them.)
- The color Palette
- Style of Line – Hard Line, Hard Rounded, Soft Line, Soft Rounded
- Texture of stroke with the percent that you want it to appear on the stroke such as Sand, Vein, Wood, and so on
- The Thickness of the stroke (you can type number in the field and the sample of stroke's thickness will show in the Tip box.)

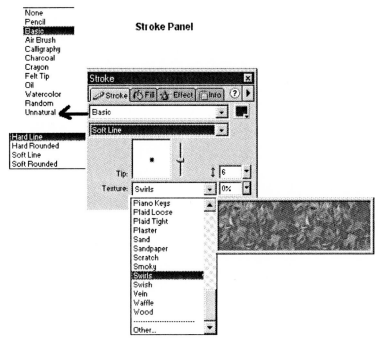

Stroke Panel

Fill Panel

The Fill Panel can be used with drawing objects, such as rectangles, circles, and others that have area to fill. You can change fills to create paths with a variety of solid, dithered, pattern, or gradient characteristics, ranging from solid colors to gradients resembling satin, ripples, or folds. Additionally, you can change various attributes of a fill, such as color, edge, texture, and transparency.

Fill Panel consist of:
- Category: Solid, Web Dither, Pattern, and Gradient characteristics such as linear, Radial, and more
- Color Palette for solid and gradient
- Edge
- Texture
- Transparency

Note: You can select the pull-down menu on the right side of each field to modify object.

To select the Solid Fill

- Chcose Solid from the Fill Category pull-down menu.
- Choose a color from Color Palette.

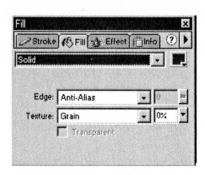

To select the Web Dither Fill

Web Dither is a combination of color that you can mix them to get a new color that may not be in the color palette.

- Select Web Dither from a category pull-down menu.
- Select color from color palette.

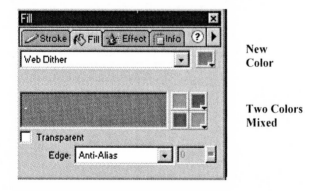

New
Color

Two Colors
Mixed

To select the Pattern Fill

- Select Pattern from a category pull-down menu.
- Select Pattern Name from a pull-down menu.

Pattern Samples

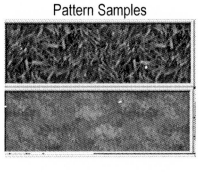

Fill panel

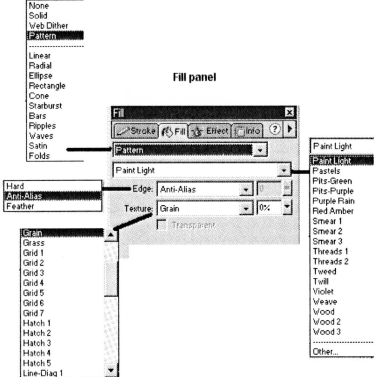

To select Gradient Fill

You can select many gradients fill from category pull-down menu - Linear, Radial, Ellipse, Rectangle, Cone, Starburst, Bars, Ripples, Waves, Satin, and Folds.

Linear 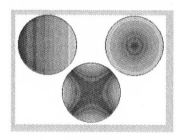 **Radial**

Starburst

Effect Panel

You can use the Effect Panel to apply Live Effects. Multiple effects can be applied to the object. When you select a new effect to the object, it is added to the list in the Effect Panel. You can turn it on or off using the check box on the left side.

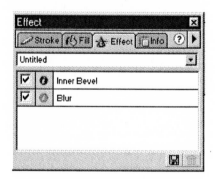

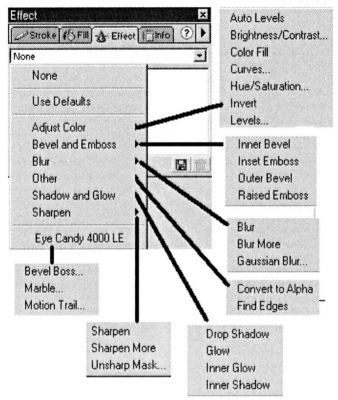

Info Panel

You can use the Info Panel to view the numerical transformation information for the selected object.

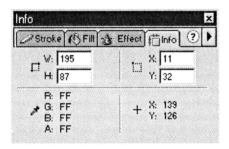

Create Vector Object with Tools

Fireworks has several tools for selecting vector objects. You can also use these tools to select text blocks, symbols, Web objects, and bitmap graphics while in Vector Mode. Selecting pixel areas describes methods for selecting pixels in Bitmap Mode.

Select Behind tool

Pointer tool ⟶ Export Area tool

To select a vector object by using the Pointer tool

- Click Pointer Icon on tools box.
- Click the object to select or you can drag over more than one object to do multiple selection.

To select
multiple objects
using Pointer
Tool

When you are working with graphics that contain multiple objects, you can use the Select Behind tool to select an object that is hidden or obscured by other objects. To select an object that is behind another object, use the Select Behind tool. You can click the triangle at the bottom right corner of the Pointer icon and click the Select Behind tool icon.

- Use the Subselection Tool to select an individual point of the object.

To select an
individual point using
Subselection Tool

- Use the Select Behind tool to select an object behind another object. You can click the triangle at the bottom right corner of Pointer icon and click the Select Behind tool icon.
- To select an area to be exported as a separate file, use the Export Area tool.

Object Panel

The Object Panel displays information and settings of a selected object. When you select an object, the Object Panel displays buttons for setting the location of the path's stroke in relationship to the vector path. However, you can set the stroke from the Stroke Panel.

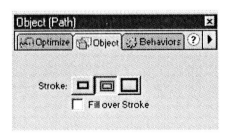

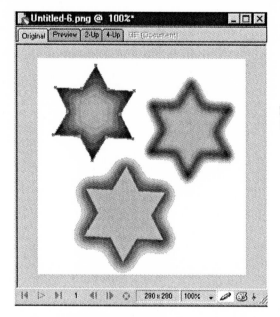

**Three different
kind of stroke path
from Object Panel**

Transform Tools

You can select to scale, screw, distorted, rotate, and flip from transform tools or choose Modify > Transform > select from pull-down menu. (See Chapter 7 Modify menu: section Transform)

There are Scale, Screw, or Distorted tools that are available in the tools box but you can rotate the selected object while you select to scale with the handles.

- Select the object
- Select transform tool from the tools box
- The handles appears

Original

- Drag the handles to transform

Drawing Tools

You can use the Draw Basic Shape tools from the tools box. There are Rectangle, Rounded Rectangle, Circle, and Polygon tools. When you select any drawing tools, you can adjust the objects using Stroke, Fill, Effect, and Info Panels. You can draw a triangle to a polygon with 360 sides with the Polygon tool.

To create polygon from polygon tool

- Double-click the Polygon icon.
- The Tool Options Panel appears.
- Select Star Shape from pull-down menu.
- Select sides as your designate.

- Set Angle (Manual or Automatic).
- Drag on the canvas.

Rectangle   **Rounded Rectangle**   Circle

Polygon (6 Sides, Star Shape)

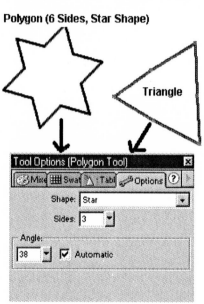

You can set Fill color from Fill Color palette and stroke Color from Stroke Color Palette.

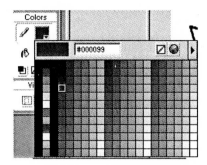

Stroke Color Palette

Fill Color Palette

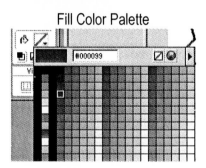

Pencil and Brush Tools

You can use the Pencil and Brush tools to draw freeform objects by dragging the pointer on the canvas. The Stroke Panel is used to adjust the Pencil Tool and Brush Tool.

- Click to select the Pencil or Brush Tool.
- Change Stroke from Stroke Panel.
- Draw on the canvas.

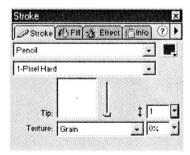

Note: You can also use pencil and brush tools in Bitmap Mode.

Pen Tool

You can use the Pen tool to draw the object by connecting points together. You can draw a straight line or a curved path segment.
- Select Pen Tool from the Tools box.
- Click to mark the starting point.

Straight Line

- Double-click the second point for the straight line to accept the line.

Curved Path Segment

- Click the second point and hold the pointer at the center of line and drag the pointer down, you will see the curved path segment.
- Release Pointer.
- Click the Pointer tool to leave the pen tool.

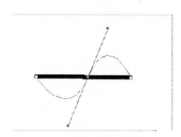 

Freeform Tool

You can use freeform tool to reshape the object's path.
- Select **Freeform** icon.

- Move pointer over the selected path.
- Drag the path.

Bitmap Object and Tools

Examples of a bitmap object include photographs from a digital camera and scanned photographs. Bitmap editing options include painting and drawing with traditional bitmap application tools, changing the color of pixels, erasing pixels, replicating bitmap image elements with the Rubber Stamp tool, feathering edges of bitmap images, cropping bitmap images, and transforming bitmap images.

If you double-click the object, the document will be switched to Bitmap Mode. When Fireworks is in Bitmap Mode, a striped border appears around the entire document.

You can select a bitmap image object with any of these tools: Marquee, Ellipse Marquee, Lasso, Polygon Lasso, Magic Wand, Eraser, or Rubber Stamp to turn the Bitmap Mode on.

To return to Vector Mode from Bitmap Mode
(Choose one option below)
- Click the Stop button located at the bottom of the document window.

- Double-click beyond the canvas with any selection tool.

- Double-click an area of the document window beyond the canvas with any selection tool.

- Choose Modify > Exit Bitmap Mode.

- Press Esc.

203

Marquee, Lasso, and Magic Wand Tool

When you double-click the Marquee, Lasso, or Magic Wand tool, the Tool Options Panel displays tool-specific options. Edge options are available for all pixel selection tools.

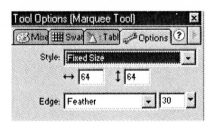

Edge

You can select the edge from the menu. Edge field has a pull-down menu that consists of Hard, Anti-alias, and Feature.

- **Hard** creates a marquee selection with a defined edge.
- **Anti-alias** prevents jagged edges in the marquee selection.
- **Feather** lets you soften the edge of the pixel selection.

Style

Style options are available for the Marquee tools only. They consist of Normal, Fixed Ratio, and Fixed Size.

- **Normal** lets you create a marquee in which the height and width are independent.
- **Fixed Ratio** constrains the height and width to defined ratios.
- **Fixed Size** constrains the height and width to a set dimension.

Marquee Tool

Oval Marquee Tool

Lasso Tool

Magic Wand Tool

Note: You can eliminate excess pixels along the edges of a pixel selection. This is useful if excess pixels appear along the border of a pixel selection or marquee after using the Magic Wand tool.

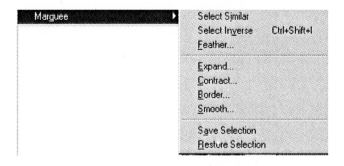

You can select from pop-up menu to modify the bitmap objects that using Lasso, Marquee, and Magic Wand tools.

Example: To smooth the border of a marquee

- Choose Modify > Marquee > Smooth.
- Enter a sample radius to specify the desired degree of smoothing.
- Click **OK**.

To select the Eraser Tool

- Double-click the Eraser icon.
- The Tool Options (Eraser Tool) Panel appears.
- Choose a round or square eraser.
- Drag the Edge Softness slider to set the softness of the eraser's edge.
- Drag the Eraser Size slider to set the size of the eraser.
- Drag the Eraser tool over the pixels you want to erase or paint over with a different color.

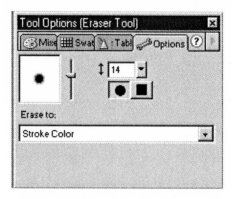

Note: you can set the eraser color in the Erase To pull-down menu that consists of Transparent, Fill Color, Stroke Color, and Canvas Color.

To remove a marquee

- Draw another marquee, or click outside the current selection with a marquee or lasso tool, or Choose Edit > Deselect, or Exit Bitmap Mode.

You can create a new bitmap image using the marquee or lasso tool.
- Select the marquee or lasso icon.
- Drag on the canvas.
- The information dialog box appears.

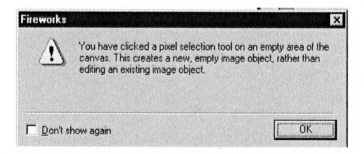

- Click **OK**.

- The Dot line around the area that you select.
- Draw using drawing tools inside the dot area.

Note: Images that you draw inside the dot border will be one unit. When you change to pointer tool, you can move them as a single image because they are draw in a Bitmap Mode inside the selected area.

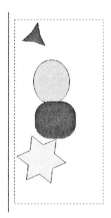

You can select Paint Bucket Tool to fill colors in Bitmap Mode. You can change color from the Fill Color Palette in the Tools box.

Rubber Stamp Tool

You can use the Rubber Stamp tool to duplicate areas of a bitmap image. When you clone an area, two pointers appear. The blue circle indicates the area you want to clone (the source), and the rubber stamp pointer indicates where you want to place the cloned area.

Crop Tool

You can use Crop tool to remove portions of a bitmap image.

- Choose Edit > Crop Selected Bitmap.
- The crop handles appear.

- Adjust the crop handles until the bounding box surrounds the area of the bitmap image that you want to keep or Drag the handles or Hold down Shift and use the arrow keys.
- To crop the bitmap image, double-click inside the bounding box or press Enter. Everything outside the bounding box is removed.

Note: To cancel the crop command, press Esc.

Summary

The Tools box (also called the Tools Panel), Object Panel, Stroke Panel, Fill Panel, Effect Panel, and Info Panel all work together. You can manage graphics in Vector Mode and Bitmap Mode using those tools. You can convert selected vector objects into a single bitmap object and any number of selected bitmap objects into a single bitmap object. A vector-to-bitmap conversion is technically irreversible, except using Edit > Undo or undoing actions in the History Panel. Bitmap images cannot be converted to vector objects. In previous versions of Fireworks, the Vector Mode is called the Object Mode and the Bitmap Mode is called the Image Mode.

CHAPTER 8
TEXT, BUTTON, AND COLOR

Fireworks has many text features that you can experiment with. You can create text by selecting the font type, style (bold, italic, underline, and more), size, colors, spacing, text transformation, and so on. You can use the Stroke, Fill, Effect, and Info Panel to manage text. You can create a text button and design using colors from the color palette.

Text Tool

You can create text using text tool from the tools box.

- Click to select text icon.
- Click in the document.
- Text block and text editor appear.
- Choose color, font, size, spacing, and other text characteristics.
- Type text (you can use enter key to go to the next line).
- Click **Apply** button.
- Click **OK** button.

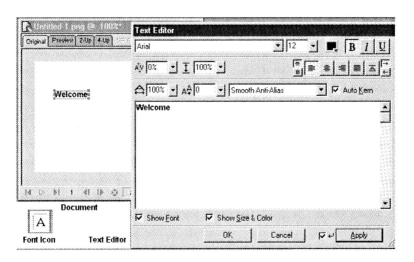

You can click the check mark in front of the Apply button to see text in the document as you type in the Text Editor. You can move a text block anywhere in the document as a single object. You can also move it while the Text Editor is open.

If you close the Text Editor and you want to return to it to edit the text again, you should double-click the text block. The Text Editor window will appear again.

Note: You can select more that one Text block to edit attributes at the same time by hold down Shift Key on the keyboard and click the text block that you wan to select one by one.

You can set the percentage of space between characters with kerning or range kerning. The baseline shift can be used to set the superscript and subscript characters. Leading determines the distance between adjacent lines in a paragraph. The Horizontal Scale can also be used to set the percentage.

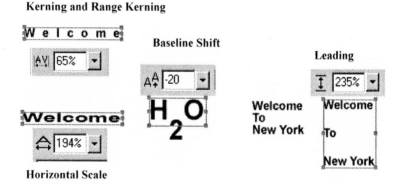

You can select the font from the pull-down menu in the Text Editor. When you move the pointer over font name, the sample font will show on the right side of the menu.

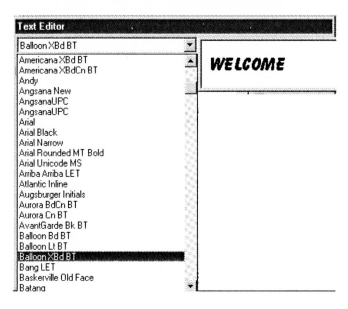

You can also select the direction of the text with the vertical text button and horizontal text button. The Text Horizontal is the default. You can also set text edges: No Anti-Alias, Crisp Anti-Alias, Strong Anti-Alias, or Smooth Anti-Alias. Alignment is also available in the Text Editor. The options are to align left, right, center, justify, and stretch text (vertical for vertical text or horizontal for horizontal text).

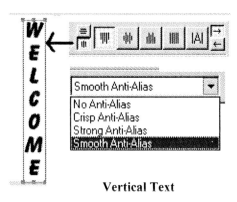

Vertical Text

214

Text can be flows Left to right and Right to left using the buttons in the Text Editor. The default is Text Flows Left to Right.

Text Flows Right to Left

Color palette and font styles (Bold, Italic, and Underline) are available in the Text Editor.

- Highlight text.
- Click Color box.
- Color palette appears.
- Select color that you want .

You can click the **B** button for Text Bold, the *I* button for Text Italic, and the <u>U</u> Button for Text Underline.

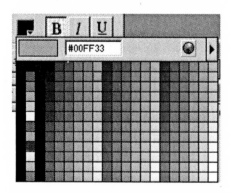

Text can be set the strokes, fills, and effects like other objects. You can export text as a text button.

Note: Thai, Chinese, Japanese, and Korean text buttons, are used as the examples in chapter 5, are created from Fireworks using the

Stroke, Fill, and Effects. You can apply one or all to the same text block.

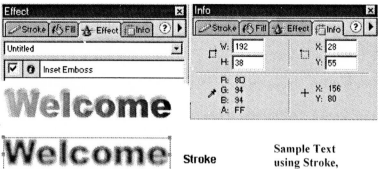

Stroke

Pattern Fill

Sample Text using Stroke, Fills, and Effects

You can draw a path and attach text to it.

- Select Path Tools (Pen, Triangle, Polygon, Circle, or Rectangle tools from the tools box).
- Draw on the canvas.
- Select Text Tool.
- Click on the canvas.
- Text Editor appears.
- Type "Welcome to New York".
- Align Center.
- Click **OK** to return to the document.
- Hold down Shift key on the keyboard and click on the path and text block.
- Choose Text > Attach to Path.
- Choose Text > Orientation > select Rotate around Path, Vertical, Screw vertical, or screw horizontal.

You can reverse direction; choose Text > Reverse Direction. You can return to edit the path and text; choose Text > Detach from Path.

Note: You should set no stroke color and no fill color for the path.

Text Button

A Text button can be created from a text block or the combination of objects (rectangles, circles, or polygon) and text block. You can apply strokes, fills, and effects to the button.

Text button (Text only)

1. Select Text tool.
2. Click on the document.
3. The Text Editor appears.
4. Type text and click **OK**.
5. Click Stroke, Fill, and Effect to apply to the text.

Text with the path (rectangle, circle, or polygon) button

1. Create text (use the step 1 to 5 as text button above).
2. Click drawing tools (select rectangle, rounded rectangle, circle, or polygon).
3. Draw on the canvas.
4. Design using Stroke, Fill, and Effect from their Panel.
5. Drag button over text block (if you cannot see the text, you have to arrange the object by send backward; choose Modify > arrange > Send backward, text will pop up on top of the object.).

You can create an object before a text block that you do not have to send backward when you drag text block over the object. You can edit the text block and the object at any time. When you click the text block, you can edit text using the Text editor, Stroke Panel, Fill Panel, and Effect Panel. When you click the object, you can modify it using the Stroke Panel, Fill Panel, and Effect Panel.

Text button Samples

Color

Fireworks provides a Filter Menu, an Xtras Menu, and an Effects Panel to help improve the colors in the bitmap images. You can adjust the contrast and brightness, the hue and color saturation, and the tonal range.

- Insert image; choose Insert > Image.
- Select Effect Panel.
- Click the category pull down menu.
- Select Adjust Color > select the option submenu (Auto Levels, Brightness/Contrast, Color Fill, Curves, Hue/ Saturation, Invert, or Levels).

Adjust Color Submenu

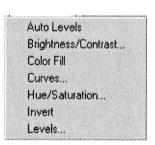

You can apply the Color Fill to blend the color over the image and adjust the percentage as your desire.

Blending Color

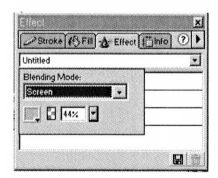

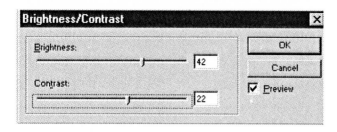

You can also adjust the color using the sliders in the Brightness/Contrast dialog box.

Original

Brightness/Contrast

Blur

Summary

You can create a document using a variety of text features in Fireworks and insert them into Dreamweaver. The Stroke, Fills, and Effect options can be applied to text and buttons. You can adjust the colors of images using the Effect Panel.

CHAPTER 9
ROLLOVER IMAGE WITH HOTSPOT AND SLICE

Hotspots and slices are used to create the interactive objects. Rollover and image maps are the interactive objects. You can create rollover images, swap images, an pop-up menus using the slice. You can also add a URL to the interactive objects in the Fireworks.

Hotspot

The Hotspot Tools consist of a Rectangle, a Circle, and a Polygon icon. A hotspot is an area of a Web graphic that links to a URL.

To insert hotspot
- Select object (image) in the document.
- Click the hotspot tool (rectangle, circle, or polygon) and Drag over the image.

Note: You can choose Insert > Hotspot.

- Select the Object (Hotspot) Panel.

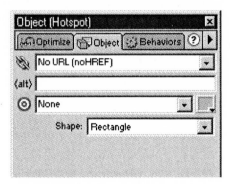

- Type URL that you want to link it in the URL field ("No URL (noHREF)" is a default) such as http://www.nyc.com
- Type text that you want to show when pointer is over the image in the <alt> field.
- Set Target page like Blank, Self, Parent, or Top.
- Set the Color of Hotspot from a Color Palette.

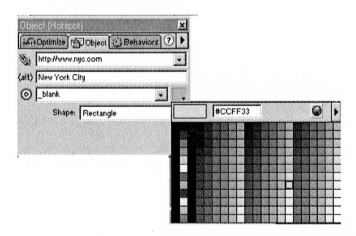

You can export them in as part of an HTML file and insert them into Dreamweaver (See details in Chapter 12). The hotspot, created with a link in Fireworks, can be used in Dreamweaver without creating any new link. You can preview to test the link from any available browsers in your computer.

Slice

Slice is a useful tool that you can use it to create the swap images, rollover images, and pop-up menu.

To insert Slice

1. Rollover Images

You should have at least two frames to create a simple rollover image, but the images should be the same size so that they rollover at the same spot.

- Select object (Image).
- Choose Insert > Slice or select slice icon from the tools box and drag over the image.
- The Slice shows.

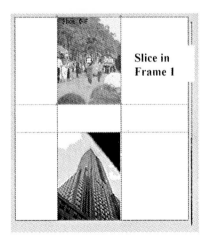
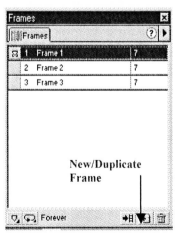

- Click New/Duplicate Frame button on the lower right corner of Frames Panel to create a new frame.

- Click Frame 2 in the Frames Panel.
- The frame 2 appears in the document.
- Choose Insert > Image and resize to fit the slice that show on the document.

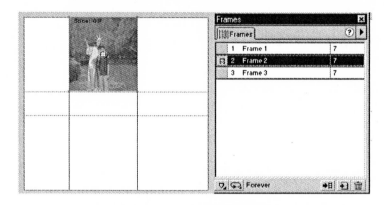

- Select the slice image in frame 1.
- Select Behavior Panel and click Add (+) button.
- Select Simple Rollover in the menu.

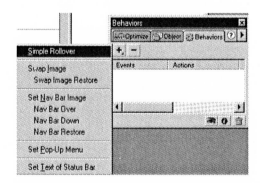

- OnMouseOver Event with Simple Rollover show in the Behaviors Panel.

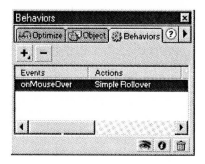

- Click Preview tab to preview (when you move pointer over the image, it should change to the image in the frame 2.)

2. Swap Image

A disjoint rollover image can be created with the Swap Image command. The simple rollover image usually has two images on the same position. When the pointer is moved over the original (first) image, it is a rollover to show the second image. When the pointer is out, the original image is restored.

When you create a swap image, two images can be placed in a different position. The concept of rollover is the same but the second image is show at the different position. Slice must be applied to both images (the original and swap image) before you create the link.

- Select the original image.
- Choose Insert > Slice.
- Select Frames Panel.
- Click New/Duplicate Frame.

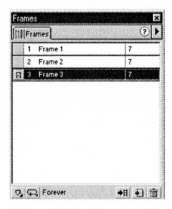

- Select Frame 3 in the Frames Panel (you will see all slices that you already made before).
- Choose Insert > Image.
- Select image and place in the document (the position of image can be any where in the document but it should not be overlap with others because when the image is swap, it will not look nice.).

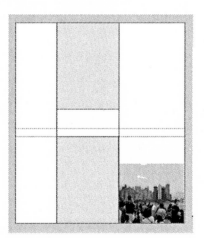

- Choose Insert > Slice.
- Click Frame 1 in the Frames Panel to return to the original image.
- Select the original image.

- Select Behaviors Panel.
- Click Add (+).
- Select Swap Image from Menu.
- The Swap Image dialog box appears.
- Click the slice in the swap image dialog box to select the swap image.
- Select Frame 3 from the Frame Number pull down-menu.
- Click **OK**.

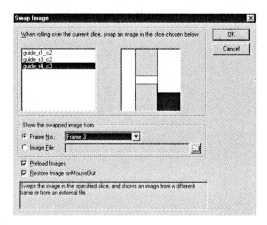

- The link between those two images appears.

- OnMouseOver event with the swap Image action in the Behaviors Panel shows.

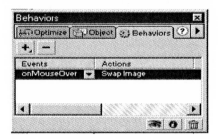

- Select Preview tab to preview the swap image.

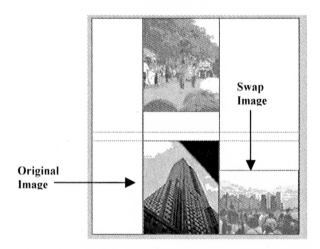

Note: You should see the image in frame 3 when you move pointer over the original (first image). You can swap the text block with the image. For example text block is the original image. When pointer is moved over the text block, the image appears on the right side of the document. You can swap between two text blocks.

Text
block
with the
swap
image

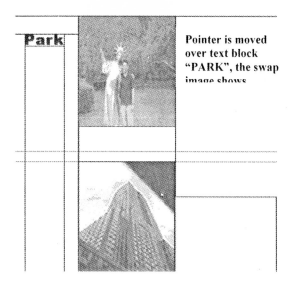

Pointer is moved
over text block
"PARK", the swap
image shows

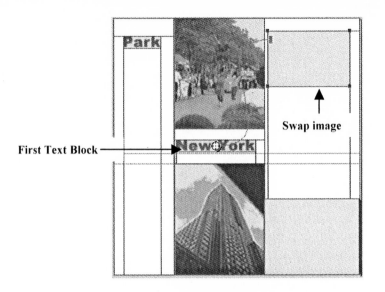

First Text Block ———————→

Swap image

Note: You can link between two slices by dragging from original image to the swap image. The Swap image dialog box appears. You can select the frame that swap image stores and click **OK**.

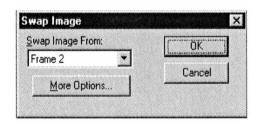

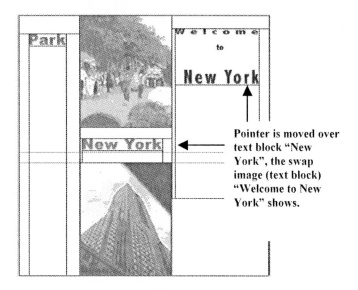

Pointer is moved over
text block "New
York", the swap
image (text block)
"Welcome to New
York" shows.

Pop-up Menu

A pop-up menu is a menu that you can arrange the sub-menus in a table cell. When the pointer is moved over the pop-up menu, the submenu appears so you can select from the list. Each submenu can be linked to a specific URL address. You can edit the font, size, and colors in the Set Pop-up Menu Wizard.

- Create and select the image or button.
- Choose Insert > Slice.

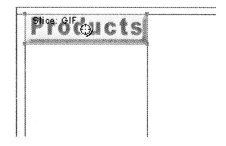

- Choose Insert > Pop-up menu.
- The Set Pop-up Menu Wizard appears.

1. Type menu item in the text field.
2. Select Target (Blank, Parent, Self, Top).
3. Type URL in the link field (if you don't know yet, you can edit them later).
4. Click Add (+) to insert the item to the list below (Click Delete (-) to remove the item from the list.
5. Repeat step 1 – 4 for more items.

You can select item that you want to edit and after you change (item, or URL), you can click change button to update your changes.

To indent or outdent

You can create submenu-using indent. To return to the previous position uses outdent.

- Select the item and click indent or outdent button.

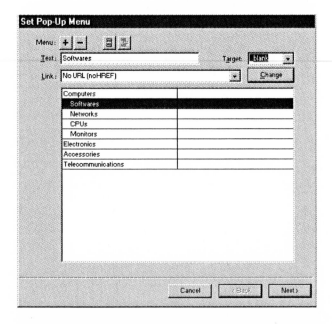

- Click Next button.
- The second page of Set Pop-up Menu Wizard appears.
- Set font type, style, size and color.
- See sample from preview.
- Click **OK** to return to the document.

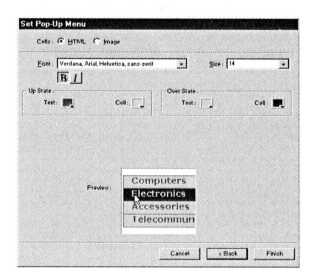

If you want to edit a pop-up menu after it is created, you can double-click the link table (blue table). The Set Pop-up Menu Wizard will appear again. You can change items, enter the URL, and edit font and colors from the Set Pop-up Menu Wizard.

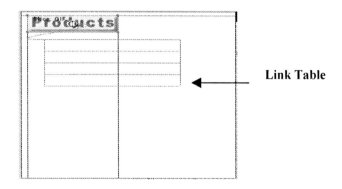

Link Table

234

You can export them as an HTML file and preview them in a browser to test the pop-up menu.

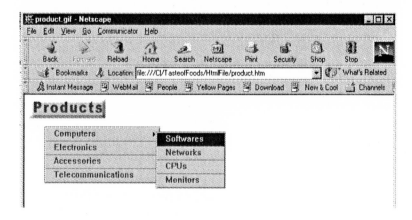

Summary

A hotspot works well with a simple rollover image. Slice is desired for use with the swap images and the pop-up menu. The images in a Fireworks application can be added to URLs to link with HTML pages. You can export them as HTML files and preview them from browser.

CHAPTER 10
ROLLOVER BUTTON AND ANIMATION

Rollover Button

A rollover button is useful in Web pages because visitors know that they can access other pages via a rollover button. You can create a new button or a new symbol by choosing Insert > New Button or New Symbol.

Another choice, you can create image and text block (see chapter 9: text button), then:

- Choose Insert > Convert to Symbol.
- The Symbol Properties appears.
- Enter name for the symbol.
- Select Type "Button".
- Click **OK**.

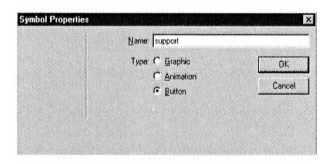

Note: The button is added to the Library Panel.

- The button (Symbol) editor appears (Up state is a default page).
- The text and rectangle (or other drawing shape) can be edited separately.
- Copy the symbol (both text block and image).

Note: When you create a symbol for the other states, the text and size of the symbol should be the same. The colors and effects can be added to another state.

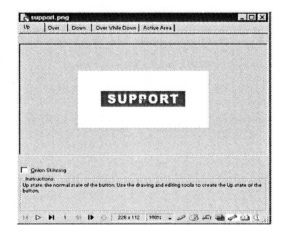

- To create the Over state; click the Over Tab.
- Paste the copy of symbol from the up state (you will get the symbol the same size and the same position as the up state.
- Set Colors and Effects for Text and Rectangle.
- Click the close (X) button on the top right corner of the Button (Symbol) Editor.

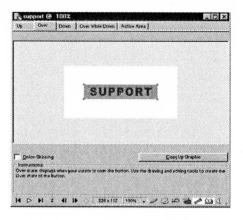

The button will show on the original document and the rollover behavior is added to the Behaviors Panel. You can click the Preview tab to see the rollover button.

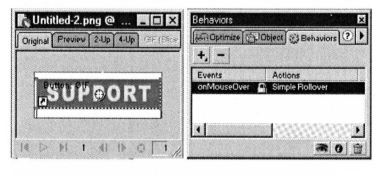

Up State   **Over State**

Note: You can insert the buttons (without setting the URL) to Dreamweaver because you can apply one button on many pages and each page you may link to different URLs.

Animation

Animation can be fun to play with and make your Web pages more interesting. The Animate and Symbol command in the Modify Menu is applied to create the animated graphics. Frames are created as your designate the number of frames. The movement can be determined from the Animate Dialog box. You must prepare graphics and put them in the Library Panel.

Note: You can create your own images to test the animation.

Using Animate Command

For example: Butterfly can fly from one side of canvas to the other side and butterfly has to swing the wings. You need to have 2 styles of butterfly (see images below).

Prepare Images

1. Choose Insert > Image.
2. Select image.
3. Choose Insert > Convert to symbol.
4. Enter name for the symbol.
5. Select type "Graphic".
6. Repeat step 1 to 2 for others.

Graphics are added to the Library Panel.

You have to create 2 frames because butterfly have 2 stages and cannot be seen at the same time. Flame 1 is always created with the document (default).

Note: Flowers that show on the document (Frame 1), you can copy and paste them to all frames later if you want the flowers to show all the time or you can create layer and paste it in layer one (background).

- Drag Butterfly1 from Library Panel to the document (Frame 1).

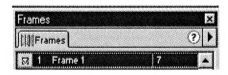

Note: Time delay on the Frames Panel (on the right side of the frame number) should be set before create others that you do not have to set each frame individually except you want to set different time delay for each frame.

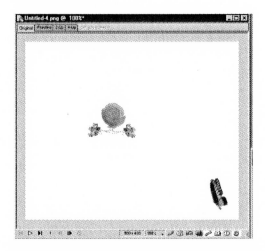

- Click New/Duplicate Frame from the Frames Panel.
- Select Frame 2 from the Frames Panel.

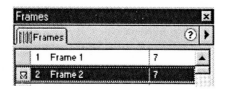

- Frame 2 appears on the canvas.
- Click the **Onion Skinning button** on the lower left corner of Frames Panel.
- Select **Before and After** command from menu.

The Onion skinning

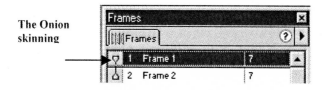

- Drag Butterfly2 from the library Panel to frame 2 at the same position as the butterfly1 (Using onion skinning to see the position of butterfly1 in frame 1).

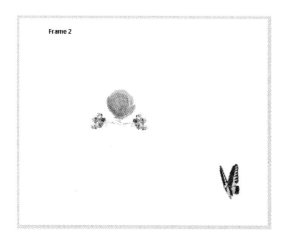

Frame 2

- Drag the pointer over both images (Butterfly1 and Butterfly2 to select.
- The handles appear.

- Choose Modify > Animate > Animate Selection.

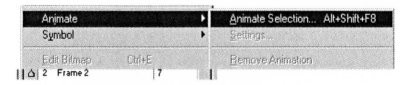

- The Animate dialog box appears.
- Enter number of frames, movement, direction, scale to, opacity, and rotate (if any).
- Click **OK**.

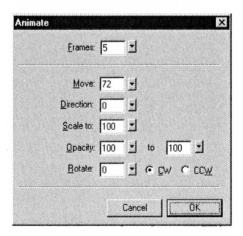

- The motion path appears in the document.

You can change the direction of the motion by dragging the motion path the direction you desire. The green dot on the motion path (on the butterfly in Frame 1) indicates the starting point. The red dot at the other end is the end point of the motion. The blue dots on the path are frames in between the start and end frame. You can drag the path close to the starting point to reduce the length of path or drag the path further from the ending point to increase the length of the motion path.

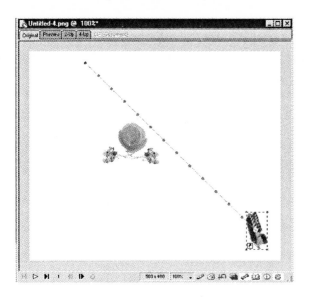

The numbers of frames with the motion are added to the Frames Panel.

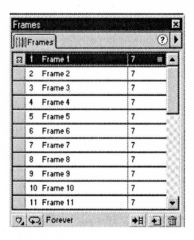

You can use the Frame Controls that appear at the bottom left of the document window. You can click the play button on the Frame Controls to see the movement of the images.

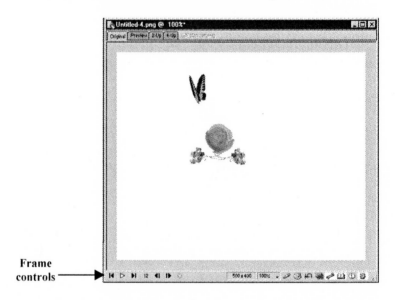

Frame
controls

When the motion path is short and the scale is set below 100, the image moves close to the starting point and scales down. When you set the loop to the frames, the image will scale down and scale up after it returns to Frame 1.

245

Sample Image with the shot length of motion path

Welcome To New York

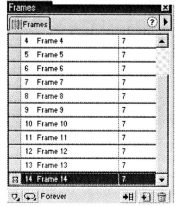

Welcome To New York

Note: If you want to create the animation of two or more images, you have to select those images at once.

Frames Panel and Animate window of the sample above

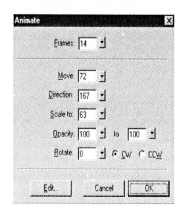

Using Symbol Command

You can use the symbol command to create tweening, a traditional animation term that describes the process in which a lead animator draws only the key frames while assistants only draw the frames in between.

- Create image and convert to symbol.
- Image appears in the Library Panel.

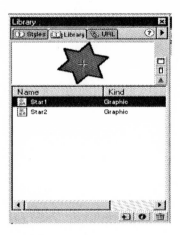

- Copy image and place to another position on the
  document.
- Click Transform (Scale) tool from tools box.
- Scale the selected image.
- Select both images (hold down Shift and move pointer
  to click another image).

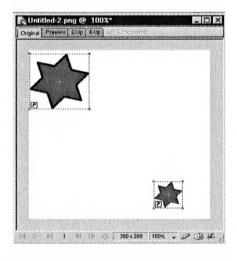

- Choose Modify > Symbol > Tween Instances.

- The Tween Instances dialog box appears.
- Enter number of steps and select the Distribute to Frames.
- Click **OK**.

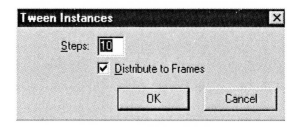

- The numbers of frames are created in the Frames Panel.

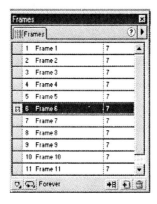

- Frame 1 appears with one image (another image will be place at the last frame (or last step).

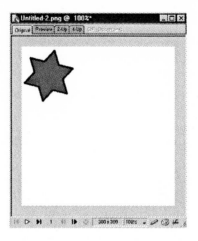

You can preview animation from the Frame Controls by clicking the Play button. The image will scale down while moving to the last frame.

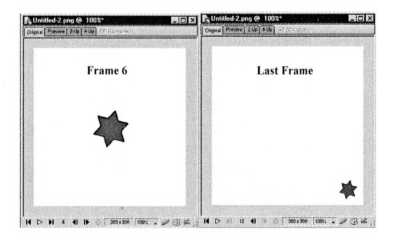

Frame 6   Last Frame

Summary

Creating animation in Fireworks is easy to do. When you Save As the animated GIF, you can insert it as a regular image in Web pages. A visitor will see the animation from your site and they won't have to download any plug-in to see the animation. The roll-over image is always exported with slices. You have to add frames

249

to create the animation. To create the tweening, you have to determine two images (the same image using copy and paste) and
create frames (choose Modify > Symbol > Tween Instance) in between them by using the Transform Tools, such as Rotation and
Scale (the second image must be scale). You can also use the
Frame Controls to preview the animation.

CHAPTER 11
DREAMWEAVER AND FIREWORKS TOGETHER

Dreamweaver is the application that can be used for managing, creating, and being a platform of Web pages. You can design the structure; create a layout, and insert objects, text, and media objects into pages. However, Web pages will not be appealing to visitors without graphics. Dreamweaver cannot be used to create or design graphics. You must prepare graphics from other applications to be ready in your site. Web pages are the rooms in the house without furniture. You can paint the walls (background), build a layout, and have necessary elements, such color and text, but it won't be enough to make your rooms look attractive to visitors.

The Fireworks application can help you design and create the furniture that you want to put in the rooms (Web pages). Fireworks is the application that you can use for creating; designing, and producing Web graphics and animated graphics. When you create Web graphics from Fireworks, they are compatible with Dreamweaver. Dreamweaver and Fireworks offer an integration feature that allows you to use both programs together and still be able to edit Web pages and graphics.

Export Graphics from Fireworks

Graphics that you created from Fireworks can be exported as a GIF file and HTML file to be used with Dreamweaver. You can use the Export Wizard to guides you through the export process and suggests settings.

To export an image and the animated graphic from Fireworks

You have to select the file format (Animated GIF) for the animated graphic in the Optimize Panel before export it.

252

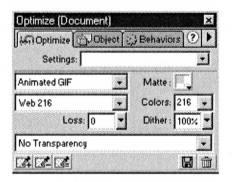

- Choose File > Export.
- Export dialog box appears.
- Select location to store image file (it should be in the folder within the local site of your Web pages that you create in Dreamweaver).
- Enter a file name.
- Click Save.

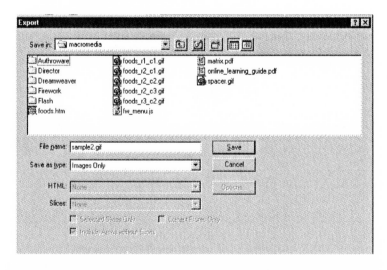

Note: you should save fireworks file (PNG file); choose File > Save or Save As, before export it as a GIF or HTML file because you can

253

return to edit the PNG file from Fireworks at any time. You can export again over the existing file name or the new file name.

To insert an image in the Dreamweaver's document

The document in Dreamweaver application must be opened to insert the image.
- Choose Insert > Image.
- The Select Image Source dialog box appears.
- Enter file name.
- Click Select.

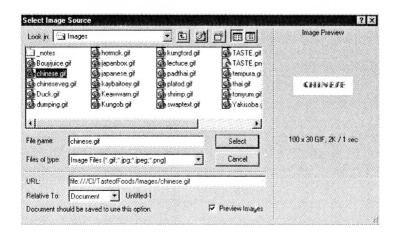

ment. The image is inserted to the selected location in the document.

To export the Rollover images and image maps

The Rollover images and image maps contain slices. You have to export as a HTML file with slicing options.

- Choose File > Export.
- The Export dialog box appears.

- Enter file name.
- Click **Save** button.

Note: The Save as type, HTML, and Slices are the default of the rollover image. You don't have to change type and options.

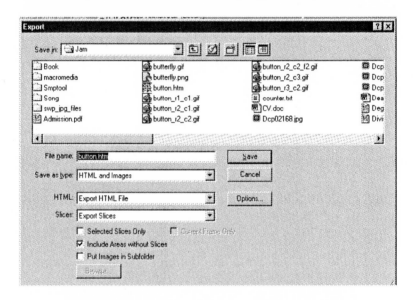

To insert the Rollover Image in the Dreamweaver's document

- Choose Insert > Interactive Images > Fireworks HTML.

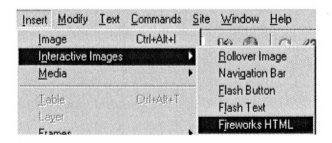

- The Insert Fireworks HTML dialog box appears.
- Click Browse to find a rollover file.

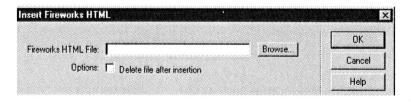

- The Select the Fireworks HTML File window appears.
- Select the rollover file (HTML file) from folder.
- Click **Open** button.

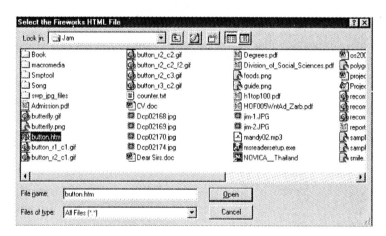

- The Insert Fireworks HTML dialog box appears with the selected HTML file.
- Click **OK**.

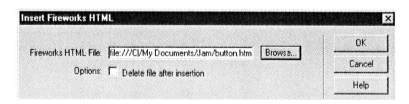

The HTML file is inserted in the Dreamweaver document. You can preview in the browser to see the rollover image.

256

Note: The HTML file and slices must be in the folder within the Dreamweaver local site because they are related together.

To export the animated graphic using the Export Wizard

You can use the Export Wizard to guide you step by step through the export process. You can select an export format or optimize a target file size (the Export Wizard optimizes the exported file to fit within the size constraint you set).

- Choose File > Export Wizard
- Select the option in the Export wizard (page 1) dialog box
- Click Continue

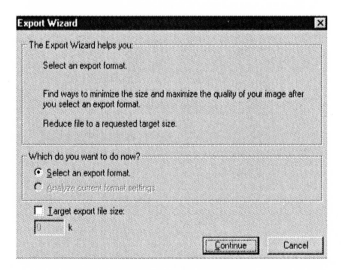

- Select the frames options from the Export Wizard (page 2) dialog box
- Click Continue

Note: The Export Wizard is helpful for the Animated graphics that you create with frames. You don't have to set the optimize Panel. When you answer the questions on each dialog box, the Export wizard set the optimization for the graphics and you can edit from the Export Preview window.

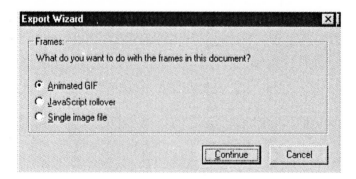

- Export Preview window appears
- Edit the setting on the left side of the window and test from frame controls on the lower right corner of the window.

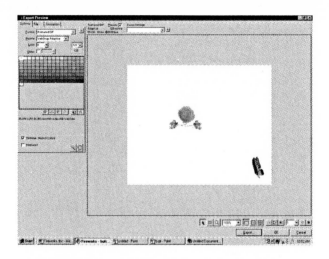

The Option is a combination of the Optimize Panel and Table Panel. You can also optimize the image using the Optimize Panel before export the image.

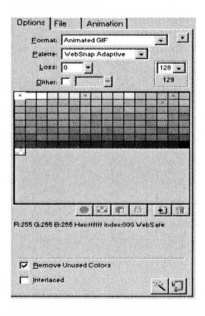

You can click File tab to set the scale, width and height. The Animation tab contains the number of frames in the document.

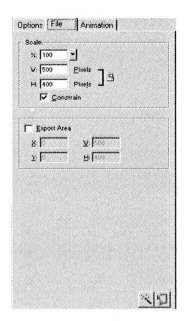
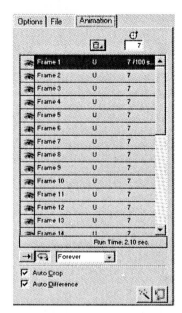

- Click Export button from the Export Preview window.

- The Export window appears.
- Enter file name.
- Click Save.

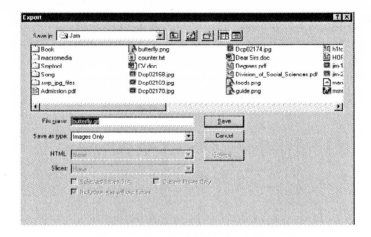

- Insert in the Dreamweaver document; choose Insert > Image (in Dreamweaver Application).
- Preview to see the animated graphics.

To export the rollover image using the Export Wizard

- Select the rollover image.

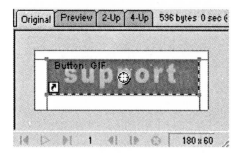

- Choose File > Export Wizard.
- The Export Wizard dialog box appears.
- Choose Destination (select Dreamweaver).
- Click Continue button.

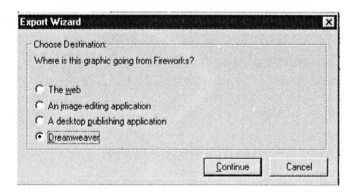

- The Analysis Results displays.
- Click Exit.

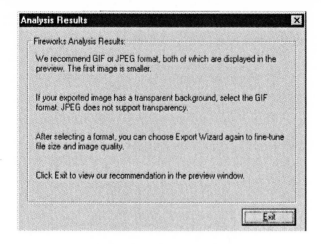

- The Export Preview appears.
- Click Export button.

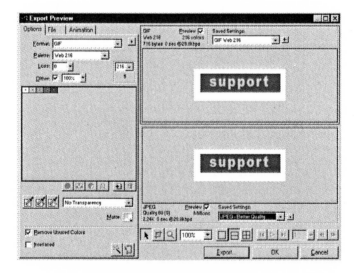

- The Export window appears.
- Enter file name (select folder in the local site).
- Click Save button.

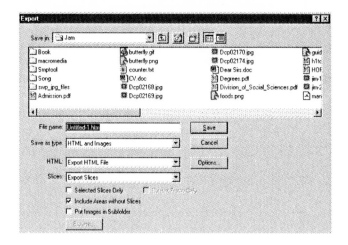

You can edit Fireworks images that insert in the Dreamweaver document using property inspector.

- In Dreamweaver, click to select the Fireworks image in a document.
- Click Edit button in the property inspector.

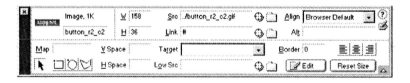

- If prompted, specify to launce a source Fireworks file (PNG file) for the placed image
- In Fireworks, you can edit the image.
- Click **Done** in the document window to finish editing (it is updating the GIF file that used by Dreamweaver and saves the PNG source file if you select to edit the source file.)

Summary

Images and animated graphics can be created in Fireworks and exported as GIF Files. You can insert an image in the Dreamweaver document by choosing Insert > Image. To export rollover images as HTML files with slices, you must insert the interactive images by choosing Insert > Interactive images > Fireworks HTML. If you are familiar with optimization setting, you can use the Export command in the Optimize Panel to export animated graphics. You can also use the Export Wizard to guide you on the optimization setting. You can also edit a Fireworks image by using edit in the Property Inspector. You can edit an image in the Export Preview window in Fireworks from Dreamweaver by choosing Commands > Optimize Image in Fireworks.

INDEX

S

save all 82
save frames and frameset files 82
save, save as, save as template 31, 32, 142, 143
scaling 168
scan 143
select all 36
select cells 73
select gradient fill 193
select rows or column 72
select the entire table 72
select the eraser tool 206
select the pattern fill 192
select the solid fill 191
select the Web dither fill 191
set image properties 95
set remote site 127
set up a new site 24
site 50
site planning and design 18
slice 159, 224
snapping layers to grid 79
straight line 201
stroke 180, 189
styles 181, 204
swap image 226
swatch 181
symbol 169, 246
system requirements 15, 131

T

table 181
test and publish the site 126
text 91

text button 217,218
text field 96
text menu 49,174
text tool 212
toolbar 37,179
toolbox 52,786
transform 172,197
trim canvas 166
tweening 169

U

undo 35,145
undo steps 148
ungroup 173-174
up 42
update HTML 144
URL 181

V

vector 132
view menu 36,152

W

W and H 96
Web design and development 6
Web management 7
window menu 51,176

X

xtras menu 176

Printed in the United Kingdom
by Lightning Source UK Ltd.
109194UKS00001BA/28